PENGUIN BOOKS

# THE UNREASONABLE FELLOWS

Nikita Singh is the bestselling author of six novels, including *Love@ Facebook*, *Accidentally in Love* and *The Promise*. She has co-authored two books with Durjoy Datta, titled *If It's Not Forever . . .* and *Someone Like You*. She has also contributed to the books in The Backbenchers series. She was born in Patna and grew up in Indore, from where she graduated in pharmacy. She is currently based in New Delhi, where she works as a publishing manager at a leading publishing house. Nikita received a Live India Young Achievers Award in 2013.

With a library stocked with over 12,000 books, she is a voracious reader and adores her collection of fantasy novels. She is a cricket enthusiast and enjoys a good cardio workout.

Myshkin Ingawale is the CEO and co-founder of Biosense Technologies, an award-winning health-care start-up focusing on point-of-care non-invasive diagnostics. His work has been featured on TED, BBC, CNN and other notable international media. In the past, he has worked at Mckinsey & Company and been a researcher at MIT's SENSEable City Lab. He holds an FPM (the Fellow Programme in Management, equivalent to PhD) in Management Information Systems from IIM Calcutta and a BTech in electrical engineering from NIT Bhopal. He remains a passionate but somewhat deluded Liverpool Football Club fan. He is also easily tempted by anything with wheels.

# THE UNREASONABLE FELLOWS

## NIKITA SINGH WITH MYSHKIN INGAWALE

PENGUIN BOOKS

An imprint of Penguin Random House

PENGUIN BOOKS

USA | Canada | UK | Ireland | Australia
New Zealand | India | South Africa | China | Singapore

Penguin Books is part of the Penguin Random House group of companies
whose addresses can be found at global.penguinrandomhouse.com

Published by Penguin Random House India Pvt. Ltd
4th Floor, Capital Tower 1, MG Road,
Gurugram 122 002, Haryana, India

First published by Grapevine India Publishers 2013
Published by Penguin Books India 2014

ISBN 9780143422211

Typeset in Adobe Garamond by R. Ajith Kumar, New Delhi
Printed at Repro India Limited

*This book is dedicated to
everyone who dares to choose an unreasonable path*

# CONTENTS

# AUTHORS' NOTES

I THINK of myself as neither particularly unreasonable, nor particularly melodramatic. Yet, six weeks in the summer of 2011, spent in the company of twenty-five extraordinary people, in Boulder, Colorado, changed at least the second bit—and dare I say it—even the first bit. In May 2011, I was not supposed to be in Boulder, where a group of social entrepreneurs from around the world had assembled, to rub shoulders with each other, to learn and to teach, have their most cherished perspectives challenged and their ventures dissected. This was the Unreasonable Institute, a one-of-its-kind business incubator for ventures, each of which had the potential to change more than 10 lakh lives each. Each venture was represented by one of its founders—who were from all corners of the globe.

This was the institute's motto—a quote by G.B. Shaw:

'The reasonable man adapts himself to the world. The unreasonable man persists in trying to adapt the world to himself. All progress, therefore, depends on the unreasonable man.'

This unreasonable place was a place where I was not supposed to be—I was only here by accident. As the co-founder of a healthcare start-up creating a revolutionarily simple medical device for India, my mind was still in Mumbai, with my team of doctors, designers and engineers. I was here only because of Abhiraman Vishwanathan (an employee who was only with us for three months and thereafter left to pursue his dream of a career in the Indian government's civil services) who did the hard work of submitting an application—mostly on his own, and mostly without my knowledge! And he had authored it in the name of Dr Abhishek Sen, a fellow co-founder of Biosense, who was all set to attend the institute. But at the very last minute, he was called away to his responsibilities at a hospital in India. No one else at Biosense could go. It fell upon me. And so, I packed my bags and flew from Mumbai to Denver, and on to a frat house in Boulder, which, for the next six weeks would be my home.

In those six weeks, I came to understand a great many new things about life, energy, perseverance, failure and courage. I have come to believe this: heroes are not born. They are made. They are forged by circumstance, and powered by their own will. Their destiny is not one which has been written but which they choose to write themselves. Sometimes serendipity enables them; sometimes they enable serendipity. They make mistakes. They persevere. They fail. They pick themselves up and try something else. They cry. They laugh. They go through common and uncommon ordeals. They are mediocre, great, average, extraordinary—it depends on the time of day and the lens through which you see them. They persevere.

Sometimes, they wither away, temporarily. But they never die. They persevere! Again. They are not born heroes. They may not all even have dreams of becoming heroes. Rarely do they know all things all the time. They are often clueless. They are often proved wrong. At many times in their lives, their paths are uncertain, their vision blurry and confused. But when they see a ray of light, they grab on to it and hold on. They hope. They plan. They hustle. They make things happen.

Again and again and again.

In this collection of stories, I hope to have packed as much of what I saw of the life stories of ten of the twenty-five amazing individuals who lived and breathed and ate and slept with me for six weeks in Boulder.

In the pages of this book are the stories of ten ordinary individuals and the extraordinary journeys that led them to become unreasonable, to become extraordinary, to challenge the status quo and attempt to change the world into what they thought it should become. These are early days for many of them: not all of them will achieve what they have set out to achieve. Regardless, they will always be—in my book!—*heroes*. They are the ones who stood up to be counted, who took a shot at changing the world. These are their stories.

Myshkin Ingawale

~

WORKING ON this book has been one extraordinary experience, to put it mildly. I have always preferred writing fiction—having the power to bend the story whichever way I please, having complete control over every single word. Non-fiction is another matter altogether. When I started, I was apprehensive; I didn't know if I could pull it off successfully. But when I began listening to the recorded interviews, I saw a whole new angle to it all—my job was to listen to all these inspiring stories about these amazing people who have dared to choose a path less travelled and stuck to their decisions, eventually creating tangible change and impact around the world.

As I listened to the life stories of one entrepreneur after the other, I got more and more excited about writing this book. Stories have always been fascinating to me and I have a habit of finding them everywhere. Someone can randomly mention how their neighbours relocated after living next door for a decade and I can build a whole story in my head about how it was for them—picturing the wife being relieved about not having to deal with a leaky faucet any more and the child being sad about moving away from his best friend. So when I took up this chance to chronicle stories of these ten Unreasonable Fellows, you can imagine my excitement.

Myshkin had already interviewed each one of them and recorded the audios. He had even transcribed a few stories, when he invited me to join in the project. After the initial apprehension I felt, not having dealt with non-fiction before, I jumped in. We were facing a deadline (I never fail to find myself in such situations) and I worked at my top speed to get this done.

One after the other, each new Fellow's story took me to a different part of the world; a different issue was picked up every time and was dealt with in a different manner. The experience was exhilarating. And of course, I'm already looking forward to repeating it, looking for people to do the next set of interviews with!

I feel strangely connected to all these Fellows, even though I have never really interacted with any of them. We're all friends on Facebook and I've got in touch with each of them regarding some aspect of the book or another, through email, but I've never met them, or even had a phone conversation. (In fact, I remember when Myshkin invited me to join in the Skype conversations he had set up to get updates on the Fellows' ventures, I had asked him to go ahead and do it without me just so I could say this here, when I write the author's note!) Anyway, so what I mean is that I've heard their voices for hours and hours on end and listened to their stories—right from when they were born till where they are now—and, in the process, they have shared their deepest thoughts. It's impossible not to feel a connection. And I say this in a very non-creepy way! More than anything, I have learnt a lot while working on this book and looked at a series of social and environmental concerns intimately. It has improved my awareness towards a lot of issues around us and I do hope it'll impact the readers of this book in a similar way. And of course, the way each Fellow has struggled, failed, given up and tried again till they succeeded is motivating. The work they are doing is admirable and we have taken up the responsibility to let people know about it. Here are the journeys of ten entrepreneurs from around the world, whose unreasonable attitude is changing the lives of millions.

Nikita Singh

# 1

# CLEAN ENERGY

SANGA MOSES

Sanga Moses—CEO, Eco-Fuel Africa (EFA)—is a devoted social entrepreneur who has committed himself to bettering the lives of his countrymen. His vision is to provide clean, inexpensive cooking energy to all Ugandans while improving socio-economic outcomes and reversing deforestation. He is fluent in all major Ugandan languages and gets along famously with anyone he meets, Ugandan or otherwise. A former corporate accountant, Sanga is a graduate of business administration at Makerere University, Kampala, and has started three successful enterprises before EFA that currently employ over 120 people in Uganda. Moses is a TED Fellow, 2012, a Community Solutions Fellow, 2012, an Unreasonable Institute Fellow, 2011. He is a mentor and a source of inspiration for many in Uganda and around the world.

SANGA MOSES was born in a small village in Western Uganda during the Civil War in the early 1980s (he does not know exactly when, and there is no written record that he is aware of). His parents—Twagira Joseph and Nyangoma Loy—were cattle herders, and belonged to a tribe called the Hima, closely related to the Tutsis tribe. He grew up in the village, learning how to tend to and milk cows. Sanga's family owned about thirty of them. When asked about how his monetary background was growing up, he says, 'Rich and poor are relative terms—I wouldn't say we were poor by the local standards. We always had a lot of milk!'

The elders in his village did not value education. 'You cannot blame them,' says Sanga. 'They had never been inside a school and had no idea what it was all about. To them, it was important that children learnt their way of life, their traditions . . . I was supposed to get married early, to contribute to the life of my community.'

So it was that Sanga never actually went or made any plans to go to school—it was only his next-door neighbour, a few years older, who took him there one year at the start of a term. He wandered into the nearest classroom and sat down, trying not to attract attention. No one—certainly not the teachers!—noticed. The classroom happened to be the second grade, not nursery, where he was supposed to start from. Incredibly, Sanga just kept attending this class for the rest of the year, without anyone noticing that he hadn't attended any of the lower grades. He struggled in the beginning, but managed to recover slowly and eventually did well enough to get promoted to the next grade. To this day, he has not got to learn formally what the rest of the students were taught in the lower grades.

So does Sanga think this incident had any impact on him? Apparently not. He got the last rank in class in the first test he took, but his grades steadily got better.

> 'Sometimes you can catch up—it doesn't matter where you begin.'

Extraordinary!

Sanga grew up quickly. When he was in the fifth grade, he started his first business: selling milk.

He would get up earlier than anyone else and fill up a set of jerry cans with the milk his family's thirty cows generated. Then he would make his way to the trading centre of the village and be amongst the morning's first sellers. Then, he would carry whatever inventory was left over and take it to school to sell it to the schoolchildren. The school was six miles away.

In school, he was known as the 'milk boy'. The bigger boys would sometimes bully him, take his milk, but, overall, Sanga managed, and managed well.

He soon realized, though, that selling to school kids is not the best business.

Why?

'Bad trade,' says Sanga. 'School kids never have a steady source of cash. A lot of them bought the milk on credit. Sometimes I would get paid weeks after I had sold the milk.' Or in the case of the bullies, not at all!

The best customers were at the trading centre, and there, Sanga developed a list of loyal customers with whom he did regular business. He ensured his inventory was sold every morning at the trading centre.

Sanga remembers very little of the lessons taught but he does remember how his school uniform made him feel! 'Putting on a uniform in the morning was great! Because back home, you would put on a sweater—and that is that. Maybe you didn't even have a pair of trousers. But now I had trousers and a shirt. Didn't mind about the shoes, because no one at school had them!'

He didn't learn much from his teachers, but dealing with his 'customers' in class taught him a great deal. 'The kids were from different tribes. I learnt a lot about how to deal with them all. In hindsight, I think it was a great learning experience.'

He didn't have any particular dream but knew he had to go further than primary school.

The secondary school was farther away from his home, not even in the same village. The school was a few sub-counties away from home and Sanga won a scholarship from the government to study there. He had to leave home and stay in a boarding school, near the Lake Mburo National Park in Uganda.

Things were different there. Sanga couldn't sell milk here,

being away from home. But he did have to do something for a living. To earn money, he set up a second business: haircuts! He started a barbershop.

Did he know how to cut hair? Where did he get the money?

'Luckily I had some money saved over from my milk business, but not enough. My mother sold a goat and secretly gave me the money to buy the things needed to set up the shop—the rent, the chair, the mirror . . . Cutting hair is not difficult. I learnt by visiting other barbershops and watching them work.'

Business was great. His fellow students liked Sanga's barbershop!

The problem was the teachers objected to Sanga missing classes to go run his shop. So Sanga had to hire his first employee—who would run the shop when Sanga was in school.

'Sometimes he would rip me off! He was older than me. Sometimes he wouldn't turn up . . . I had to make sure things were running well and pay real good attention to the money. It was difficult to manage on weekdays, because I had to be in class. The best I could do was pay extra attention to the business Saturdays and Sundays . . .'

Sanga did okay. 'I was actually a rich boy!'

How much did he make?

'I used to make about 10,000 Ugandan shillings . . . about four US dollars every week.'

Not bad for a school kid!

Sanga bought himself a pair of shoes and still remembers the day with pride. 'I became a *king*! Shoes!'

Sanga's exploits earned him the respect of his mates in

school. His friends used to call him 'Da Investa' (the investor).

Did he think about setting up a second or third barbershop?

'No,' says Sanga. 'I looked at this as a subsistence business. I didn't look at it as a business at all. It was just something that kept me at school, helped me buy books and generally kept me happy.'

In the higher classes—secondary school (senior three), he got introduced to his favourite subject: *accounting*. The subject was taught by a Mr Mugisha Dawson, and Sanga loved the subject! No one related to it like Sanga in his class. He would pay rapt attention and relate it to what he was doing right and wrong at his barbershop. He gets animated as he talks about this, 'The first time the teacher came and taught accounting, I was like—*wow*! It was the first time I enjoyed class. Because they talked about money and . . . you know? I was so happy! I finally had something in school I loved.'

At this stage, Sanga had big dreams. 'I dreamt of going into politics, of becoming President. You see, everyone in school looked up to me . . . I was always given positions of responsibility—I would be the head boy, the class monitor, and I had so many friends. It went to my head!'

But Sanga's dreams changed after school. Sanga went to Makerere University Business School to study business administration (BBA). An experience there changed his views about politics.

Student elections there were heavily politicized and were a big deal. Sanga became close to the ruling party student leadership. He was the chief mobilizer for the campaign. While there, he observed things and ended up writing a book—about the National Resistance Movement (NRM), the party of the President. It was titled *Why Uganda Still Needs Museveni*. President Museveni liked it, and invited Sanga to visit him. He incurred the jealous wrath of many intermediaries in the party. Sanga met the President, who offered to buy his book for 20 million Ugandan shillings, which is about US$10,000. The President signed the cheque but Sanga never got the money.

Why?

'One of the President's men—a big man in Ugandan politics—took the money. It never got to me.'

The President was seeking another term in office and that is why he bought Sanga's book. The NRM used the book as a campaign tool. They published chapters from it in newspapers and gained publicity. But the President had signed the cheque, so Sanga doesn't blame him, but the experience turned him away from politics. He saw the real, corrupt face of the politics in his country.

Sanga had invested about $500 in the printing, and incurred a large loss. His first big loss in business! Learning many lessons, he finished his three-year course in business administration, majoring in accounting.

With a friend from his university, Musopa Ahmed, he started another business—compiling and publishing 'pass-paper' notes for students. 'We effectively started a printing press. We would get the material and print it. Students wanted the notes to prepare for exams. It became very popular.'

It did well, but was destined to remain a small business, not enough to sustain both of them. Musopa and Sanga decided to look for jobs. 'We decided that whoever got a job first would join it and leave the business to the other. Incidentally, I got a job first and let Musopa continue with the printing press.

'The job was that of a front desk officer at a microfinance company—the Uganda Finance Trust. In the first year, I worked at the front desk. In my second year, I moved into sales. In my third year, my boss said, "Why are you doing sales? We need someone who is good at accounting and finance!" So I was relocated to finance and I finally became an accountant.'

Sanga worked at the head office, in Kampala. 'I learnt a lot. I enjoyed the work.'

By this time, it was 2009 and Sanga was regularly sending money back home to his parents and sister.

One day, on the way back home to his village, he met his twelve-year-old sister. She was carrying a bundle of firewood on her head. When she saw Sanga, she started crying. 'I remember it was a Wednesday. My sister said she had also missed school on Monday.'

His sister told him that she had to skip school often to go hunt for firewood. It broke Sanga's heart to see her toiling for so little. There was no wood in the village because of deforestation and his sister had to spend a lot of time going in search of wood for fuel from places some distance away. His sister said, 'You can't leave me here. Find me another job. I am dying and no one back home can help . . .'

Now, Sanga did not know anything other than accountancy. 'I didn't know anything about climate change, or deforestation or nothing. But when I saw everybody telling me how hard it is and how much they struggle back in my village, I started researching about possible alternatives to wood fuel.

'In my quest to find out more about it, someone referred me to Dr D'Silva. He was a professor at the university I studied in, and comes from one of the South American countries. He was the head of the renewable energy department. So, I went to him for guidance and he gave me a pile of data about how to make sustainable clean energy from biomass and the idea of biocharcoal came to my mind. And I was like—I now have a solution. What am I doing here?'

Sanga resigned from his job immediately. Now he had this dossier—a file full of ideas from Professor D'Silva. The idea had taken birth inside him and he knew what he wanted to do next. But how did his boss react to the out-of-the-blue letter of resignation?

'I went to my boss and I told him, "I'm resigning." And he, was like, "Are you out of your mind? We have invested a lot of money in training you. What is it? Have you got another job? Is this about salary?" And right there, he offered to double my salary to make me stay in his company. I refused, but he didn't budge. My resignation was not accepted.'

His fiancée also considered the doubling of his salary a very good opportunity. So, seeing no other option, Sanga stayed on with his company for another month. But he could not sleep at nights. He was sure he was making a very big mistake. So eventually, he went to his boss for the second time and this time, he managed to get his resignation approved.

'An idea had taken birth in my head and I knew that not letting it grow was going to be the biggest mistake of my life. Forced to stay at my previous job, I could not sleep. I had nightmares every night. I knew I could not continue my job any more.'

'When I quit my job, I had only US$500 in hand . . . and I needed at least 10,000 to start a business. So I had to work out how to manage with the meagre sum of money I had.'

He met Ben Tandekwire, who had gone to the same secondary school as Sanga and was working for a local NGO as a community development officer. Upon listening to the idea, Ben agreed to contribute some money to help him. He did not quit his job to work with Sanga full-time (since they did not have enough funds for his salary), but became a co-founder of the company.

The good thing was that the house Sanga was renting just outside of Kampala (Sanga remembers that Kampala was too expensive for them to afford, and the place they were operating from was close to a sugar-cane plantation, which aided in providing them the agricultural waste, their starting material) had some spare space. He built a small shed outside and hired four guys. That was their office—they could operate from there. The things they invested in were—building that shed, making a kiln, a bicycle and paying the hired hands.

They started collecting agricultural waste. They made charcoal powder from agricultural waste, but they did not have enough money to convert it into actual charcoal that could burn in the stove. They did not have the machinery for the compaction. So instead, they used their hands to mould it into a slightly more compact form (as compared to the loose-powdered form).

'Well, it worked. But it didn't work well. Because it was only hand moulded, when burnt in the stove, it became ash. It just wasn't strong enough. And that was our big problem.'

Luckily enough, it was around that time that the government began to realize that these people were doing something good. That was when Sanga became aware of the $10,000 grant issued by the government to help people like him.

'When I went to meet with one of the government officials and told him about our work, he showed interest. That officer suggested that I apply for the grant. It was like a business plan competition organized by a group of entrepreneurs, working under the government, called the Private Sector Foundation. It helped private entrepreneurs.'

That campaign, sponsored by the World Bank, came as a blessing for Sanga and his business. They applied for the grant and won it!

Their first advance of US$5000 took them places. They built a factory, bought proper machinery, hired more people, trained more distributors—the business reached a peak.

'Remember, we were going to get another $5000 from the grant we won? We never received the balance sum. In developing countries, you can never be sure! But the money we did receive helped us build a sustainable business model.'

So they had reached the point where everybody could see

that their idea actually worked. The charcoal was perfectly good, the distributors were happy and they were on their way.

Their starting material is agricultural waste—sugar-cane waste (bagasse), coffee husk, rice husk. These materials are usually available at farms and agro industries. So, Sanga's company leases their kiln to the farmers and the agro industries and train them how to turn their agricultural waste into charcoal powder.

Then, Sanga's company, EFA, buys the charcoal powder from them at four cents per kilo.

This powder is then transferred into another machine they invented—a solar-powered machine that converts this charcoal powder into cooking fuel. This cooking fuel is compacted charcoal that can burn at high temperatures without turning into ash too quickly.

'We have a team of young people with bicycles and another team of distributors who have kiosks in their local areas. The kiosks are like small retail shops in rural areas and small townships. These kiosks are operated by women. Our boys transfer our charcoal on bicycles to these kiosks and sell it to those women at seventeen cents. These women then sell it to the final consumers at twenty cents.'

Their business provides a means of living to a lot of people. The kiosks are sometimes established, and at other times, they provide an opportunity to new people to get into business.

'We go to several areas and call for people interested in distributing their charcoal. Some people are already in the business of selling wood and others are new to the business. So we interview them and take them through the process, training them to work efficiently and equipping them with some basic business skills. And we request them to make an initial investment in the kiosk. If they already have one, it's good—it means they are already doing business selling something or the other. If not, they start one.'

At present, EFA supplies to about fifty kiosks.

'We have not been that consistent. Because, sometimes, the sun is not reliable and we cannot produce enough charcoal. But, on average, in a day, we are making about 500 kilos. So, that's about 15,000 kilos a month.'

Fifteen thousand kilos of charcoal, created from agricultural waste sounds impressive, even considering some of it (an average of fifty kilos) gets spoiled in the process during drying.

Sanga is still not making more money than he was making in his job. Putting together the business and scaling up has cost a large sum of money. And most of the money they make is then reinvested in their business, so there is not much left.

'I've not been paid for about four or five months!' Sanga laughs.

The company is called Eco-Fuel Africa Limited and they have two goals.

'One of which is to provide 40 million Africans with clean, affordable and sustainable cooking energy made from agricultural waste. The other is to plant at least a quarter of a million trees by the year 2020.'

So, where does he want to see his company in the future?

'Everyone has realized that this idea works. So, we have received so many requests from other districts for us to set up factories in their areas, doing the same. So our aim, at the moment is to grow, be able to afford better machinery, make our business model efficient and then, we'll sell franchises to people who are interested in our kind of business.'

So, instead of managing every small factory in every area, they want to empower local people to manage the factories themselves! It will be a cost-sharing thing—they will request interested people to contribute a percentage in the initial set up and then they will bring in the technical know-how and retain a small percentage of the company.

This is their plan of scaling up, which will be much easier than expanding on their own.

So, do they expect a lot of interest from other businessmen in this business?

'The sub-Saharan Africa faces the same problems. So, whoever knows about our business will want us to go and work in their country, so I think this model will help us to scale up.'

The biggest challenge EFA faces right now is the inefficiency of the machinery they use. The machines they use need to be stepped up. They produce fifty kilos of charcoal per hour and when they work for long durations (say ten hours in a row) the machines fail to take the load, because of being overworked.

This is not really surprising, given that the machinery they use is partly assembled locally and the parts are bought from Asian countries like India and China. The frames, et cetera, are fabricated locally and one of Sanga's friends, who is an engineer, does the assembling of the machine parts.

Apart from slightly inefficient machinery, funding is the

other problem EFA faces. 'Depending on the amount of money we have, we are now operating at our full capacity. But we know that this is not the best that we can do. The demand is increasing by the day. Uganda has a population of 30 million people, which depends on firewood and charcoal fuel. That's a very huge potential market.

'We are now serving one village with about 5000 people, so you can see the extent of the untouched market.'

Right now, EFA does not have enough money to invest in the infrastructure or the machinery required to cover the entire market. So yes, they need investors.

But Sanga is very confident about that as well. They have a solid business model and they are contributing to bettering the lives of their countrymen. Their vision is to provide clean, inexpensive cooking energy to all Ugandans, while improving socio-economic outcomes and reversing deforestation. And he knows that they will find several eager investors.

In 2011, Sanga applied to the Unreasonable Institute and his venture was taken up, on the basis of Eco-Fuel Africa's potential and their performance in the year 2010—launching in 2010 with only US$500, Eco-Fuel Africa had already brought clean cooking fuel to over 3500 energy poor families in Uganda, created over 1500 jobs and replanted over 12,000 trees in Uganda.

So, something that originally started with wanting to help his sister get cooking fuel easily has come a long way! How is the sister doing now, we are tempted to ask.

'You see, in my family, there is a slight problem. In our

community, they marry off kids at a very young age. My sister was supposed to be in school, but my mother found a man for her to marry. Now, she is out of school and the wedding is about to take place very soon.'

His reaction to this?

'I do not approve of what they do, so they do it behind my back! But at least they have charcoal in the village now!'

Sanga bought his family an improved stove and he makes sure they have charcoal all the time.

Apart from their present business model, do they have any other vision?

'Of all the charcoal powder made in different ways, we have realized that our charcoal powder actually works well as an organic fertilizer. It improves soil fertility when added to the soil. And in contrast to other fertilizers, our charcoal powder stays in the soil and works for a very long time.'

So currently, EFA just teaches farmers how to make their fertilizers but they are now exploring this area, too. If they can find a way of mass producing fertilizers and selling them to people, there is more business in the offing. So EFA is thinking about that. Maybe, Sanga wonders aloud, in a few years, they will also be one of the biggest manufacturers of organic fertilizers in Africa. That plan is still in the research stage, but they may diversify into this field in the future.

Sounds great!

We like the way every business plan that takes birth in Sanga's head is always safe for the environment, when the alternatives used for them today are anything but.

Throughout this journey, what has been going through

Sanga's mind? What has been his personal philosophy in life? What is the essence of Sanga?

'Trying the impossible,' he says, proud of himself. 'And catching up, of course!'

> '*Whenever* you decide to begin anything, *wherever* you may come from . . . some things are seemingly impossible. But if you have a dream and you have faith in it, everything is possible.'

'I could never imagine that I would go to a university. Because no one in my village ever went to one. And then, when I came to this Unreasonable Institute—that's another story.'

Sanga's business is based out of his home town. When he decided to start his business, he relocated from Kampala and went to a rural township, because that was where they could find the agricultural waste they needed as their starting material.

'There was no Internet there. I had to go to Kampala, which is about seventeen miles away, to get access to the Internet. Secondly, I didn't know anyone with a credit card—in Uganda, we do not have credit cards. And the only form of payment on the Internet was through credit cards.'

So there were a lot of obstacles in his way, when Sanga began to set up and scale up his business.

'Everybody told me, "Why are you wasting your time? Who is going to give you the money?" But guess what—I was one of the twenty-five people to get funding. That is how far a dream can take you.'

He ends with, 'Sometimes it looks like it is not possible, but like I said, if you have a dream and enough faith, everything is possible.'

## What's New?

There have been many wonderful changes in Sanga's life and work since I last spoke to him. Eco-Fuel Africa now benefits 30,000 people. Its network has 2500 farmers, which includes 1000 women. It has created 260 women retailers, each one earning up to $115 per month. Eco-Fuel Africa won the Tech Award in 2012. Sanga was named a Community Solutions Fellow, 2012. He is now a married man and has a beautiful one-year-old daughter.

# 2

# POWER TO THE PEOPLE

Donna Morton has been involved in the social sector for nearly thirty years. From being arrested while working for Greenpeace and building campaigns for NGOs to starting numerous organizations and working for the US think tank Sightline Institute, she has done it all. Recently, she has provided consultation services to businesses, governments, NGOs and numerous First Nation and aboriginal business organizations. Her expertise includes communications, economics, social enterprise start-ups, partnerships, economic development and film-making.

She is the CEO and co-founder of First Power, an organization that aims to provide access to green energy technology along with jobs and economic benefits to First Nations and other communities. She was selected an Unreasonable Fellow, 2011, for building one of the world's best social innovation start-ups. She was also awarded the Ashoka Fellowship for her work with the Centre for Integral Economics (CIE). CIE encourages social and environmental sustainability through market-based solutions.

Donna has gained popularity and visibility by speaking, and sometimes delivering the keynote address, at various events including the Business Alliance for Local Living Economies (BALLE), Bioneers, VBN, arts, health, women's and policy organizations. She has done extensive media coverage including the Canadian Broadcasting Corporation's (CBC) budget commentaries. She has been featured in the press in the *Financial Post*, *Globe and Mail* and numerous magazine articles as well as in radio interviews.

DONNA GREW up in a very high-crime district in Toronto, which she remembers as being nice. Right from the beginning, she got a chance to mix with people from diverse cultures—only 20 per cent of the population of the school she went to was Caucasian.

'I grew up with a very strong sense of the world. Despite growing up in Canada, I had friends from India, Pakistan, Africa, Greece, Italy—literally from all around the world, and we were the closest of friends. That was truly a gift.'

Donna's family had been in Canada for many generations, with a very working-class mentality. They were not a family with too many aspirations. As Donna says, their mindset was like, 'We are workers, we keep our heads down, we don't fight the system, we don't try to change things, we are lucky to have a job.' They did aspire to be good and kind human beings, but bringing change was not in the fabric of her family.

Her father was a low-end salesman and her mother a secretary. Donna got her ambitions and her sense of purpose from immigrant families. It was in the Korean, Italian and Jamaican families around Donna where people had dreams for their children. They also had more education than Donna's family. No one from her family had ever gone to a university.

Someone once told her that she was smart and should go to a university. That was the first time Donna thought she had it in her to make it into a university. She used to think that if she really stretched and worked really hard, she could some day become a hairdresser—that was her highest ambition before then. But she was motivated by the Korean families around her to have an ambition and a purpose in life.

'It actually became difficult for my family that I became ambitious and wanted to step outside of our place.'

Donna had never been a very good student, mostly because she had never strived to be one. But when she thought about going to a university, she got serious about studies and begged her school to let her get on to the university track. It was her first battle—the first time she had wanted anything enough to fight for it. Once they agreed, she put her head down and started to work hard.

'By this time, I had realized that there were people out there who spent their lives trying to change the world. Till then, I had no exposure to Gandhi or Martin Luther King, but then I saw a movie called *If You Love This Planet*. It was a film made in my country by the National Film Board, and it was illegal in the US. After watching that movie, all of a sudden, I had a strong affinity to these people. I remember having a very profound sense of purpose from that moment on. I was inspired by seeing a doctor use her education to fight for justice. I wanted to do something like that.'

The first step was going to a university. In her high school, only forty students graduated to go to a university. In her neighbourhood, Donna saw some of the brightest kids around end up in prison. Donna says it was because they were so bright and entrepreneurial but their energies were not channelled or directed to the right path to use their talents and creativity.

But Donna had a spark in her, which she wanted to ignite.

She studied art at university. It was a very conservative school, and there were people of great affluence. She mixed several classes in her course, to make it a very liberal degree—fine arts, literature, drama, film, philosophy, economics, classical studies and such. She received grants to pay for her education.

Did she, at any stage till then, think about making big money?

'Not really,' she says. 'It's not my motivation. It doesn't thrill me at all. What thrills me increasingly, is contributing in some way with my life to justice. I have known that ever since my teenage years—that's my driver. I knew what would make me happy.'

In her early twenties, she worked on activism and on raising money for Greenpeace.

'I had the privilege of actually knocking on doors of every economic stratum in my country—ranging from the extremely rich to the extremely poor. I discovered that some of the most miserable people I ever met lived in huge mansions, while some of the most self-content, generous, happy people lived in housing projects, on very little money. I learnt that the sense of completeness, self-satisfaction and happiness has nothing to do with your earnings.'

After her liberal arts BA, she looked for something to do a master's in and found a programme in film theory at New York University, which interested her. She was just starting to look at possible scholarships, when she came across a book—*The*

*Brantley Report*—which had a profound impact on her and she decided to take a summer, or probably a year off from academics and work for Greenpeace instead.

She joined Greenpeace in 1989 and finally felt like she belonged somewhere. She was amongst people who were on the same wavelength as her.

'I felt like an alien. When I was shaken by the impact of a movie or a book, I felt like a very dramatic alien. But when I went to Greenpeace, I stopped feeling like an alien. They were a group of people who were ready to put themselves on the line to say, "No." To say, "This is not acceptable."'

It was a time when people were not very concerned about things like nuclear weapons, the risks of nuclear power, toxins and such. It was around that time that the Bhopal gas tragedy and the Chernobyl disaster happened. She was shocked at what humans were capable of, at the atrocities against people and animals and the life-supporting mechanisms of the planet. She felt like she had to do something.

Donna started as a fundraiser for Greenpeace, and then got promoted to running an office where she was managing substantial funds. Then she got recruited by what they call 'the action team', which is a band of activists who drive boats, hang from the bridges, chain themselves to oil-drilling vessels and the like. She became one of those people.

> 'I went to jail roughly every five weeks for two years.'

Her new lifestyle was very disconcerting to her family. They had a strange, dramatic daughter who never fit in anywhere, never kept her head down, being a good little worker like everyone else in the family. They were just beginning to come to terms with the fact that she had gone to a university. They had begun to think that she was going to be a doctor or a lawyer, or do something to lift the family name. They were just beginning to accept all this, when she dropped out of university and began getting arrested on a regular basis.

Eventually, her family came to be very supportive, but they could not handle it at that time. In those years, it was very upsetting for them.

Donna worked on a series of campaigns for Greenpeace. She worked on the anti-nuclear campaign, for which she drove/co-piloted boats, spread radiation symbols on aircraft carriers as large as 7000 personnel aircraft carriers.

'When the water cannons hit you in the head, it hurts a lot. They hit your head against the side of the boat and you shake like a rubber doll.'

So what was the experience of working there like?

'Literally, it's a little bit like a very small special forces squadron. We were all connected with radios and it really felt like a military op. I was also a part of some of the espionage teams, so I would go and spy on the military bases and learn their weaknesses—like when the shifts ended, where the lowest fence was, which area was the least protected—anything to help us enter. I would go there in a little sundress, with my sketch pad, and pretend to be an art student. I would go, "Oh! Look at these beautiful shadows and lines, can I come in and draw?" And I would be let in. By engaging people there in conversation, I got to know about their shift changes and other stuff that would help us get in later.'

She did not fear getting shot at, being sent into prison—nothing! At no point did anything overpower her will to work hard to make a difference. She was hell-bent on the path she had chosen, and she was in no mood to deviate.

But that does not mean she did not get scared every once in a while!

When she was twenty-two, she wrote her will.

'I wrote letters and documents to my family—in case something happened to me or I went to prison—trying to explain what I was doing and why. It was very real. All those things were real; I could have been killed. I could have been sent to prison.'

Donna feels that on the inside Greenpeace is a machine—a very sophisticated messaging, communication, operation and fundraising machine. But she had a lot of love and admiration for the people she worked with, so it did not really matter.

> 'For the first time, I had a tribe, a community of people, which felt the same way as me. I was accepted there.'

Donna got a lot of media training and became a good spokesperson, along with being a good spy. She was also very good at getting arrested! When the cops would arrest her, she was never disrespectful to them. She told them how much she admired them because they were trying to protect their community and standing up for their beliefs, just as she was. She sometimes had very beautiful and profound experiences with the police who arrested her.

Their jobs were inherently in conflict, but she never insulted them, never felt the need to turn them into monsters. Unlike most of her peers, who saw the cops as 'dirty pigs', as they put it, Donna knew the problem was in the system, not with the cops to whom she could shift the blame.

If given the chance to relive those years, Donna would jump at the chance!

'I never got shot at, but I got arrested on a regular basis, got attacked by helicopters, sometimes carried and stuffed into paddy wagons, not very nicely, sometimes even put in jail with people who really could have hurt me a lot.'

She could have moved up the ladder at Greenpeace, and she had several offers to do so, too, but she somehow felt like she was 'done' there. She felt like she had learnt enough—as if she had graduated—from there and it was time for her to move on, to do something more constructive.

At twenty-four, she went back to Canada, and started a youth organization that spoke on behalf of future generations. They taught thirteen- to eighteen-year-olds to believe in their power to speak about the environment, but also about the jobs and the economy. So, Donna's scope had really expanded and that was exactly what had been her limiting factor while working with Greenpeace.

'While working with Greenpeace, I had started to realize that whenever we came into conflict with workers, I felt as much for the workers as I did for the planet. I didn't take their side *over* the planet, but I felt like I could empathize with the police, I could empathize with the workers and I had begun to empathize a little bit even with some of the businessmen, whom I didn't see as demons. But inside Greenpeace, it's hard not to demonize, especially the corporate executives, but something was expanding in my thinking and I needed to do work that demonstrated that expansion.'

Her organization was called GRYFFIN, which stands for Group Representing Youth for Future Interests Now. She founded it with a good friend of hers—Zane Parker—in the year 1991. They basically trained young people in British Columbia to find their voice and believe in themselves and what they cared about and honour that. But also to take responsibility to speak for future generations.

'We taught young people to understand the concept of inter-generation equity. That was really our key principle. We believed that if people are unfair to each other now and live with dramatic global disparities—north and south, and even within countries across strata—then by being unfair and unkind now, we are being more brutal to the future.'

They were doing good work—integrating sustainability, economics and jobs with the future generation. There was a lot of complexity in what they were trying to do.

'I have always been very drawn to complex projects.'

All this while, she was just managing to support her expenses. She would support her activism with waitressing, something she had done to put herself through university, too. She says she always knew she would never starve because she could pick up a tray, go out and make a few bucks.

Eventually, she learnt how to raise money. Her organization got some funding from the government, because the government got interested in the work GRYFFIN was doing, and in a good way! That experience was different from what she had had in Greenpeace.

In two years, Donna felt like she was 'done' again. There was a group of people in the Green Party, who liked the work she was doing in GRYFFIN. She had a lot of mentors such as a former World Bank economist, Michael Mascall, who called her one day and told her that he was recruiting for the next federal election and wanted her to run as a candidate.

In 1993, she got recruited by the Green Party of Canada to run as a candidate in the federal elections. Donna was twenty-six, and at first, she was unsure about it. But then, they became persistent and involved a lot of other people—people who would back her—who assured her that they had some campaign money, a campaign manager and that they believed in her talent.

It was the South Vancouver Island federal ridings and she was running to be a member of Parliament. It was very early in the Green Party's history in Canada, and they had never got more than one per cent votes. But somehow, Donna felt drawn to the idea.

'Frankly, it was an amazing opportunity. It was like doing

a very condensed master's degree that I didn't have to pay for. I had all of these policy experts in all of these fields, who became my advisers. I had law professors, economics professors, agriculture professors, experts in transportation, experts in women's policy, experts in poverty—all of whom rallied around and helped me. The Green Party policy had been a bit light and there were aspects of policy that had not been developed, so we were writing policies for the Green Party of Canada.'

Quite an educational experience!

With the help of all those academics and experts, Donna drafted new policies and filled up the blanks. She became very interested in policy work and moving up. When she ran for elections, she did well. For a young woman without much experience, the 2.4 per cent she acquired was quite a feat. It was higher than anyone from the Green Party had ever achieved. She got equal footing as all of the other candidates. She was in all the candidate meetings and received equal media footage.

A man named David Anderson won the election and later went on to become the environment minister for Canada (and also signed the Kyoto Protocol). He was a very kind mentor to Donna and they are still very good friends.

After the elections, the Green Party wanted Donna to be their deputy leader, but she chose to work in their forestry department, which was one of their weakest links.

While this was going on, she got recruited by a sustainability think tank in the United States, which was an organization that came out of the Worldwatch Institute and was called the Northwest Environment Watch, now known as the Sightline Institute. It is basically a sustainability research centre in Seattle.

She worked as business and communications director for Sightline for three years. They did some really interesting communications work, integrating the threads of sustainability—economics, employment, poverty obviation and carbon taxes. That was when Donna became absolutely enamoured by the economics side of the green agenda.

She realized that in her initial experience with the environment movement, that was what was lacking—the understanding of economics. She went back to Canada and started an NGO—Centre for Integral Economics—with the knowledge of economics she gained from the Green Party and Worldwatch Institute, which she used as her basis. And then she invited academics and other experts to come in and flank them. They hired a research director, who had a master's degree in resource economics.

'People hate taxes, and my job was to make them understand that taxes are the most powerful tool that we have to align market forces with sustainability outcomes. We concentrated a lot on market mechanisms and taxes and created a lot of ground swell in British Columbia. We created a public understanding of tax shifting that led to the BC Carbon Tax. That was our big achievement.'

'We ran campaigns, and one of them, I recall, was called—Taxes Are Sexy! We had a lot of supporters wearing T-shirts saying that.'

Some people were baffled seeing that slogan, since no one ever looks at taxes as a good thing. But CIE made them realize that taxes are the most powerful tools progressives have to align everything we love with an economy that can pay for healthcare and education. They were popularizing complex policies and people were struck by that; their idea worked.

In Canada, her work was widely known and appreciated by people at the top and also at the bottom. She was excited that people from all classes could come together and meet around a particular transformational, common agenda. It held her attention and she worked on that for a decade.

After that happened, once again, Donna felt rather 'done', like so many times before. She wanted to move on to something new.

'I felt some sense of completion—that I went in for ten years and I had worked really hard. I was in my thirties, so I had a larger attention span—ten years this time!'

Towards the end of that work, CIE was awarded an Ashoka Fellowship, which was a very big honour.

Donna wanted to have more contact with people at the grass roots and their issues than she had working on policies. She enjoyed working on policies and she knew she was making a difference, but she wanted to be more in touch with the people. And that, for her, was the underpinning of First Power.

'There was an entrepreneur emerging in me. Ashoka helped me see it; I didn't think I could be an entrepreneur, until Ashoka literally knocked on my door. Ashoka was a magical opportunity to further explore social entrepreneurship and really come to understand how it functions globally.'

How did this change in her thinking happen? How did she realize that she was meant for entrepreneurship?

> 'If you look at my career, I was not making very linear decisions. I was making highly intuitive, following-my-passion decisions. And it has served me very well.'

'I don't do very well stuffed into a box. So the idea of being in a cubicle, Monday to Friday, nine to five and someone telling me that I can't do something because it is outside of my scope of work is not the thing for me.'

By this time, CIE was running quietly, doing smaller projects and Donna decided to take a break. She was farming part-time, because she needed a shift and some time to think. She was living just outside of Victoria, on an island and using the beauty of the mountains and the satisfaction of planting trees as part of her transformation period. She read a book called *Blessed Unrest* by Paul Hawken.

She had met Paul Hawken at a conference and they had become friends. He had gifted the book to her and Donna devoured the book twice—back to back. The book makes an argument that we are at a moment in human history where we have created the largest movement, which includes peace, justice, anti-poverty, housing, spirit, social entrepreneurs and all such things. If we see ourselves as one, we can have enormous power to change the world.

Around that time, she received a call from Joe Thwaites,

who was an engineer with a twenty-year experience as a renewable energy entrepreneur and visionary. He ran one of the bigger, more successful solar hot-water companies in Canada. She had worked with Joe before and had great respect for him. He had an idea in his head for which he wanted Donna to partner with him.

Donna got interested in the idea upon listening to it. They started putting together a team. They tested some pilots, the first few of which were not quite right. They set up a solar plant, when the community made them realize that it could be so much more. They went in and explored the possibilities, by finding out what the communities really needed.

When they started working with the communities, it turned out that people did not just want renewable energy and they did not just want solar hot-water systems; they wanted comprehensive renewables. And not just renewables, they wanted jobs. And not just jobs, they wanted economic development.

Remote and poor communities around the world rely on dirty and expensive diesel or other fossil-fuel-based power. After meetings with hundreds of aboriginal leaders in Canada, Australia, Thailand and India, there is an imperative to get rid of diesel generators, gain energy independence, improve health and put scarce money to better use. In the Hesquiaht language, '*Hish uk ish tsa walk*,' means everything is interconnected. We must solve energy issues while addressing poverty and climate change.

Conventional commercial renewable energy projects merely 'accommodate' communities rather than give them the opportunity to share in development, jobs and significant/ majority ownership. Communities should not be forced to choose between feeding their elders and paying for diesel heat, light and power.

That was the thought that started First Power. Their strategy to overcome these issues is to provide integrated solutions that harness renewable energy to drive job creation and economic development, while averting climate impacts.

One hundred per cent renewable energy power can be financed by harnessing the amount saved from the cost of fossil fuel to capitalize projects. When the community is involved in developing energy projects, it can then include complete solutions. The energy projects of First Power are designed in such a way that majority or complete ownership is with the community, which keeps profits in communities where they can be leveraged for future economic development.

The business model includes service fees to co-develop projects and carbon credits while allowing for fair equity in commercial projects. Unlike conventional developers, the community can always be in charge and able to meet complex needs and build pride. These projects can empower and literally create the energy to end poverty.

'The idea got developed at every step and now I realize that in its essence, we are no longer a renewable energy company. First Power is basically a community-development agency, which uses renewable energy as the way to do it.'

Helping people see the opportunities, helping them incubate, train and build capacity in people to do these things, bringing in the right financial partners and government agencies to finance and make the capital possible—First Power does all of these things. In essence, they helped the community to do planning and they raised the money to do so—from the government. The planning was funded by BC Hydro.

They ultimately abandoned solar energy and shifted to biomass, wind and micro-hydro energy instead. Joe had done a lot of policy work on renewables and his background was chemical engineering, so he had knowledge of not just solar energy, but also an excellent understanding of the technology and the entire sector.

The proposal that they took to BC Hydro was to do deep community engagement to really map with what the community wanted, to start the communication and grants-writing process and do some of the mapping about what the community would look like and how it would be structured. It is a five-year project and everything—starting from job development and training to economy development—will cost about $5 million over five years.

Donna is an Unreasonable Fellow, 2011, and believes that the institute has given her the mentorship she needed and has helped her broaden her horizons further.

'For me, success would be measured by three things. One, the green micro-grid that we are pioneering works. The second and the real complex measures of success are on the social-technology side—I want there to be a transformation inside these people. The third one is real jobs, with a sense of purpose and alignment with their culture, which will drive them into a legitimate local economy that will thrive.'

They currently have three full-time employees and ten

contractors. They have some more people (for example, people from social development, community development, planners, technical engineers and videographers) who work for them part-time, and are incredibly gifted. They capture a lot of things they do on videos to promote the project.

Their customers are usually the nation and individual tribes, which have limited access to resources. Mostly, it is about leveraging money from foundations, governments and private partners.

How big does Donna envision First Power becoming?

'It is a *for-profit* organization. We want to be a global company and transform the energy sector with what we are doing. We want to reinvent this sector.'

First Power is a unique organization that blends business innovation with social purpose.

Their vision is simple: to put green-energy technology along with jobs and economic benefits into the hands of communities.

First Power works with the Centre for Integral Economics. Through diverse partnerships, innovative planning and oral- and graphic-based communications, First Power supports communities in owning renewable energy.

They make renewable energy solutions available to First Nations and other communities. They work with communities to envision, plan and integrate renewable energy into larger goals while building conservation programmes tied to the culture. They create jobs, training and economic-development opportunities in the renewable energy industry and build partnerships between diverse sectors to provide holistic solutions to support economic and community development, fundraising and financing.

'Close your eyes and imagine yourself living in an economy where everything your local economy makes, every service, every good, is fuelled with 100 per cent renewable energy. Imagine the cleanness and how it feels.'

In the next few years, Donna is confident that they will build a model that works globally—sustainable and scalable. She does not believe in the way emerging market countries are told, 'Cut off who you are, because if you follow the traditions of your people, you will remain poor forever. Give up your old ways of poverty and jump on the modern train and we will take you to the promised land of capitalism and making tonnes of money.'

She believes that the most resilient economies are authentic, diverse and based on a depth of culture and integrity of the people inside that economy. And that's the logic she follows.

She is driven by the idea that the term 'life is not fair' is not true, and it does not have to be. She says, 'The most important thing for me is that when I am old and dying, I can look back over my life . . . I want to know that I helped make the world fairer for the generations to come. That I contributed, brought my piece of truth, my stone to the pile and my life to honouring how beautiful humans can be.'

## What's New?

'We were on *Fast Company*, we were in the *Guardian*—it has been a good year. But also some challenges—we haven't grown as fast as we wanted to. We are only now in the process of building our capacity. We have a few projects—million-dollar-plus projects. We are looking for a couple of senior project manager hires along with financial and legal hires who can put together large energy deals. And our first equity financing deal could well happen in late 2013 too . . .'

For Donna, 'business' and 'social' morph into one, seamlessly, without distinction. First Power's clients are large development agencies and First Nations' indigenous communities. In most projects, First Power aims at turning communities into surplus energy producers. 'The difference in the last year has been a change of scale,' says Donna. 'While before, our typical project would be a hundred thousand dollars, we are now looking at million-plus-dollar projects.'

A particularly memorable project has been a solar-energy installation that has also morphed into a cultural and art project. In this, a local artist from an indigenous community has taken a mural from thousands of years old cave art—depicting the operating code from the First Nations' community ancestors on how to live life—and, using special technology, has etched it on to the five solar panels that are the energy source for the project. 'It is an interesting fusion.' Donna smiles. 'Thousands of years old images applied on to a cutting-edge renewable energy technology. Beautiful piece, powerful symbol of old wisdom that exists in communities . . . We want to do more like this!'

So, ahead for Donna and her team lies more art and energy! 'And scale!' she says, emphatically, but still with her characteristic softness—an atypical combination that, of course, typifies Donna Morton!

# 3

# DON'T SETTLE

NATHANIEL KOLOC

Nathaniel Koloc is the co-founder and CEO of ReWork, a social enterprise that helps talented professionals find work opportunities at companies that have a positive social or environmental impact.

ReWork connects talented professionals with paid-work opportunities (both full-time and project based) at companies that include for-impact start-ups, non-profits and social enterprises, triple-bottom-line brands and Corporate Social Responsibility (CSR) departments at large corporations.

Nathaniel has a master's in Strategic Leadership toward Sustainability from the Blekinge Tekniska Högskola in Sweden, and a BA in Global Human Impact Studies from the University of Vermont. He's a proud member of the StartingBloc community (BOS '10).

BORN IN 1986 and raised in Pittsburgh, Nathaniel comes from a very supportive family and community. As a child, he was not pressured to go to school, but he was always taught about the importance of education and took it seriously. His mother's (Brenda Smith) work concerns public health and environmental protection. She started a non-profit organization, which is a global medical redistribution organization. She is now an executive of an organization dealing with watershed protection.

His father died when Nat was twelve years old. He was the head of the advising centre at the University of Pittsburgh. Most universities did not have a distinct advisory department; they just had professors taking care of it. But in the University of Pittsburgh—since they had too many students—they had a separate department, and Nat's father was its head.

'It's actually kind of interesting, now that I think of it. My father dealt with advising students about what classes to take, what to major in, and helped them have a perspective about their academic future. And I never made this connection before, but what I am doing is almost the same as that! I literally never, up until this moment, realized that!'

Nat's father worked at the university for thirty years. He was involved with education and believed in its virtue. He was heavily involved with universities dealing with higher education and helping people understand what they wanted to do.

'So when it came to me, my parents always made it clear that I should do what I felt was my purpose. There was no pressure to become a lawyer, or a doctor.'

It was this thought, that made him the 'explorer' that he was in school. From an early age, since there was no pressure from his parents and no chosen path, it let Nat wonder what he wanted to do and explore everything.

Nat is an only child. His father was married once before and has two children from that marriage, who are around fifteen years older to him. Nat is close to them but, because of the age difference, their relationship is more like one between a nephew and his uncles and aunts.

Nat went to a public school and had a very tight group of close friends. They were very social, but also very involved with things like Math Week and Mock Trials. They used to compete in all the 'dorky endeavours' (as he puts it) like the Science Quiz and had a lot of fun with that, until the time they started playing soccer. They used to participate in events like thinkathon competitions and compete with much better schools, even the private ones. But since they had such good chemistry between them, they used to win, even when playing against better teams.

'We were definitely not smarter than students from these other schools, but we worked really well together and had wonderful dynamics, so we would win, like *a lot* of these things!'

So along with having so much fun in school, Nat admits that he also began to understand the importance of teams.

'A team is so much more than just organizing a group of people and managing tasks. There is a whole different level to teamwork.'

Later in college, the University of Vermont, Nat never was a part of any team which worked as well as he used to work with his friends in high school. When in school, subconsciously, Nat did not realize it but the combination of the freedom to do anything he wanted to do and the desire to have fun with it set the stage for what he took up in college. It gave him an open perspective and, without feeling the pressure of doing anything specific, he chose to major in zoology.

'At that time, I thought I wanted to do marine biology. I also wanted to travel internationally, since that is kind of my favourite thing to do.'

Later, when he packed bags to travel Europe for three months, he found that going to the bars and the tourist spots just for the heck of it was very unfulfilling. He began to hate travelling without a purpose. He is still excited about travelling around the world, but not unless he has an appealing purpose behind it—studies or work.

While studying zoology, the first class of his second semester was on 'World Food Population and Development', which was basically a sustainability class. The department was a very innovative department called Community Development and Applied Economics (or CDAE). It was about all the big issues that the world faced, that even the most educated people either do not understand or pretend to not understand or maybe simply do not care about. Nat was blown away.

'It was an amazing, amazing class. I loved it. I had no doubt that I was going to work in this field. I understood that sustainability is the issue of our time. I used to be a little bit predisposed in high school—I was always a bit of an environmentalist at heart. I loved animals and nature.'

Nat was eighteen at that time. After attending that first class on 'World Food Population and Development' he designed his own major—abandoning zoology immediately and turning towards Global Human Impact Studies. He did a cross-college designed major, hand-picking all the classes that had to do with ecology and natural sciences—biochemistry, ecology, international development, microeconomics, development economics and all the ones they had on sustainability.

That comprised three years that were Nat's basic freshman, sophomore and junior years. Of all the classes, Nat was most interested in coastal ecology and got a chance to study it abroad, too, on two occasions. Coastal ecology was an interplay of coastal culture and ecology, so there has been a strong emphasis of science in his background. He always had the rigour of understanding the scientific processes and the interdependencies of ecology—studying not just mammals, but the ecosystem, too (in ecology), and not just items, but the relationships between them too.

'For semester C—which was much less academic, but involved a lot of travel—I got to go to seven different countries in Asia to study about international politics and development.'

So, at this point, did Nat have a vision of where he would be five or ten years down the line?

'I was also running the school newspaper's business department, simply to make some money. That was when I realized that I was pretty good with numbers and entrepreneurship. It felt like fake money, since it was the school's money and we were given it by the student government. So we were working with actual money and testing how to make more of it—understanding market and business operations—but with zero risk. That's where I learnt how to take risks, fortunately at someone else's expense!'

Even though Nat did not have a clear idea of what he would be doing a few years down the line, he was certainly learning a lot of important lessons on the way.

To get sponsorship for the paper—the *Vermont Cynic*—Nat and his partner at the newspaper came up with an ad-based revenue model. They changed the whole strategic plan of the paper and went for as big ads as they could get. It made sense in the beginning, but later they realized that is wasn't the best route. Getting a lot of smaller ads, which would do constant runs turned out to be a better strategy. So instead of selling a big, full-page ad space for $1000 each, they later chose to sell smaller ads for $1500 for an entire semester. That's when they started getting better response from the clients.

'When the ads had a longer run, people started seeing them again and again and it generated better output. So the products started selling more and our clients were happy. We were too, since it became cheaper per run, as we boosted the client base by about 60 per cent and completely transformed the financial system.'

By the time Nat left school, his team had brought the financial profit to $18,000 per annum, from $8000 when they first started. Nat is happy about the significant change he and his team brought about in the system there.

'The risk taking was like—*wow*! It totally showed us how much fun business could be. So, by that time, I did not know what I really wanted to do in the future, but I knew that I'd be doing something that is essentially green business. Using the mechanism and strategies of commerce, the value streams of business, in order to address the sustainability issues of our time—that was what I knew I was going to do.'

After leaving college, Nat tried to do exactly that. And, in his words, it was '*so fucking hard*' to do. He had to figure out where to go to work, which organizations were doing what, who was the thought leader, who was just talking about it—it was very complicated.

His first job was working for a one-guy consulting company in Pittsburgh, which had the same vision as Nat—doing business planning for clients and helping organizations understand sustainability. He was put in touch with the guy he was working for by his mother's network in Pittsburgh.

'There's a big environmental non-profit scene in Pittsburgh and it is a very innovative place in terms of taking initiatives for different kinds of work.'

Even though the owner of the company was a good man and had a vision for the company, Nat tells us that he was too idealistic and did not have much experience or training in the field of business. They secured some big clients and landed some high-paying deals and despite some setbacks, the company was doing well. But even so, it was clear to Nat that he needed to move on for his own professional development. From a personal-growth standpoint, he felt that he needed to advance and go somewhere else.

'He and I parted ways. This period of my life was insane. It was incredibly unstable and every day was different. I worked for eleven different companies! I worked in construction, I did strategic planning, I led youth camping trips—I mean I did everything. Such a range! The only thing I didn't do was work for a big company. Missed out on that somehow!'

Wow! Now we sure want to know more about this unstructured phase!

'I was basically extremely risk tolerant. I knew that in the worst-case scenario, I'd compromise and go get an average job somewhere. Until then, why settle?'

This whole range of jobs happened because Nat was very picky about what he wanted to do and he felt very strongly about not settling for something he didn't feel strongly about. All this time, he had essentially about a hundred dollars in his bank account at any given time and he kept taking risks. He was just managing to get by, and not complaining about it. He says it's a feat he did not have any loans.

'The higher education system is totally messed up in the

States. People have so much loans that it just cripples their decision-making and they have to compromise and go for anything that pays money for the loan. I was lucky I did not have loans coming out of undergrad.'

Apart from some scholarships that Nat received, it was essentially his parents—mostly his mother—who funded his education. He considers himself fortunate for that; he could not have taken risks with his career had he carried the baggage of a huge loan with him.

So what happened next, career-wise?

'It wasn't linear; there was no flow. It was happening in a completely haphazard manner, one after the other. I did a business-planning and grant-writing-consultant job; I did construction; Student Conservation Association—doing volunteer work for camping trips (which was awesome!); I worked for a company called Fitz Associates, which was an information design company; I installed rain barrels; I did landscaping, worked for Adventures Cross-Country, which was ecotourism for high-school students and let's see . . . eleven jobs! I used to have a list of them with me at one point of time, but I misplaced it long ago.

'See, I was literally dancing around,' he laughs. 'I was in different parts of the States, spent some time in Ecuador, Boston and . . . that's when I decided I need a career shift. I knew I'm smart, I believed in my talent and when I realized what I had been doing, I said to myself, "This is ridiculous; this just doesn't make any sense. Why isn't there an organization where I can feel good working?"'

He cared for sustainability and considered signing up

for organizations like Teach for America, where they have a shortage of employees who are good at consultancy and strategic planning. He thought he could be of use to such organizations. He knew that there are people who are working as hard as they can to make a difference and he wanted to be a part of it. He wanted to go to the frontline and get taught whatever these organizations needed. He wanted to get involved with business planning and strategic support.

With the professional experience of working with such companies, he'd also be trained to lead organizations later. In his words, 'I can have a big impact later if I can learn by having an impact now.'

So that's how the business started! The beginning of TerraShift.

'I recruited Abe to help me—he and I went to high school together and he was a part of the group which understood the value of teams and the importance of teamwork. Abe is younger than me, and, at that time, he was just finishing an industrial engineering course. But he had been doing a five-year programme, so he did have work experience with four profit operational companies before he graduated. He could see what I saw—we had the same perspective. He understood the potential, because he knew how difficult the labour market is for getting certain things done.'

How did the idea turn into an actual business?

'Abe and I realized that this was a huge deal. We knew we were getting into a lot. And to be honest, only now we were realizing that there was one more key issue—if we were really ready to actually have three to four full-time employees working for us.'

And we did notice that he had just about a hundred bucks in his account!

That did not stop them. Nat, along with Abe, started taking up projects and learning in the process. By 2011, they had made $50,000 in revenue. They just kept doing projects that they had envisioned their services being useful to. To begin with, they brought together people and built a team of a few very enthusiastic and hard-working college grads and developed a business plan. So they started testing if their plan worked, and the market supported the idea of the kind of team they had.

'They are basically subcontracting teams. I mean, it's not that crazy. But it was just a bit unusual.'

So, Nat had—from his own network—found people who were willing to give his company business on a variety of projects.

Nat decided and Abe agreed that Nat should go to Blekinge Tekniska Högskola in Sweden to get a master's in Strategic Leadership toward Sustainability. It was something Nat had always had an interest in and it would also give him a chance to learn more and help his business develop.

'It was a very, very specific, very unique course. This degree threaded together everything I wanted to do in college academically and everything I had interest in professionally. It was equal parts two things. One, understanding the system's principles that we are violating globally as a society. And two, how to bring organizations into alignment with them.'

The programme taught him how to talk to people about

sustainability and convince them that from a business standpoint it was not a sacrifice, but an opportunity. Also, that it was urgent and necessary. And finally, that it was possible and there was a way to do it. So basically, the course was a mixture of understanding the science behind it and how to make organizations understand them and work with them.

Nat was able to take the whole curriculum, everything he learnt there and apply it in his own business. While he was doing the course, he was also working for his own company, back in the States. Abe was handling the business at the time in Pittsburgh—doing more and more projects, hiring out, subcontracting and bringing other college grads in. And even though Nat was not physically present there, he was still working with them virtually—Skype, emails and phone calls. He was devoting thirty hours a week to TerraShift and forty to his course.

By doing all of this, the company developed a great portfolio.

'Basically, a proof of concept was done, while I was in graduate school. By working successfully on these projects, we had established that our idea works. We were ready to show it to someone now.'

That's when the Unreasonable Institute first came into the picture.

Before that, in the year 2008, they applied to StartingBloc, an organization which trains next-generation leaders to do good and do well. Nat found them on a competitive landscape analysis when they were first starting off. Nat found the conferences and the people he got to meet there very inspiring.

He says that StartingBloc was almost like a precursor to the Unreasonable Institute to him.

'We literally love StartingBloc. Their CEO, Adriana Pence, and their fellowships director, Sara Bishop, are on our advisory board. StartingBloc was like an amazing tribe of people. I think I have a deeper connection with the Fellows in the Unreasonable Institute because it's action oriented. StartingBloc is more conversation based. The best way to put it—StartingBloc is like dipping your toe into the water and the Unreasonable Institute is like putting your face in front of a fire hose! But they beat with the same heart; they're very much aligned.'

After StartingBloc triggered them, they started prototyping and, by that time, Nat came back from Sweden and they applied to the Unreasonable Institute. They had the proven concept and hence the ability to go and put it in front of the Unreasonable Institute and gain access to mentors and colleagues. They figured it was time to hire people and bring in other business partners.

Everything came together.

'We have our proved concept, we have our vision and we have our strategy for the next year. We can now systematically check our revenue assumptions, build our networks, increase our revenues piece by piece and we can develop our competencies. Two years from now our operations will be exactly how we envisioned them.'

That was their plan two years ago, but it took them some time to put the pieces together and in Nat's words, 'It's been a lot of fun!'

It's a strange feeling that simultaneously I feel like it has been so long and also like we have just started. It's exciting!

The experience has not been disappointing to Nat at any point of time.

We ask Nat a little more about what the whole jigsaw will look like in three years' time. What's the vision in his head—about where the money is coming from, what are the projects and how the TerraShift model is working?

'Overall, what we are doing is balancing two needs. On the one hand, we have a generation that wants to work hard and, on the other, we have all kinds of organizations, with different customer segments (impact start-ups, non-profits, corporations, et cetera), all of which stand to benefit from understanding how they can engage and develop this new generation. Now that they know the impact, they can do better work. So, our interventions are ways to channel the energy into impact organizations.

'For example—we have a project-staffing service, which does not sound glamorous, but is quite exciting actually! It's basically mini-consulting. It's a way for teams of college grads to work on business-planning and strategic-planning projects, rapid-resolve initiatives that help companies become more rigorous and disciplined.

'Another segment we work on—a full-spectrum HR [human resources] department. We help out companies that do not have the time or resources to take care of hiring and firing, doing offer letters, employee manuals . . . and basically the entire HR system. At a low monthly fee, we provide them with our HR services.

'And here's the big one—there are large corporations which want to understand impact space, innovation space and how to better engage the new employees who are emerging out of training programmes. So we take these employees and train them in our own way. For example—we take new employees from Agro Sciences and take them to Latin America for two months and show them a number of different agricultural products, doing a project about GMOs [genetically modified organisms] and vermicomposting, have them work on projects for other organizations and bring that knowledge and understanding of the entire context of the work and come back to be more engaged in their field of work.'

It's going to take their company an approximate time of eighteen months to develop. While they are doing that, their revenue is now coming from the staffing-services projects and HR systems projects. They plan to have an organized, systematic approach to sort through what might look like chaos to an outsider.

They have a lot of different ideas and Nat believes that they are no longer stumbling forward—which they were, in the beginning. When they began, they did not really know what they were doing. But they are glad that they did—that's how they got here!

They are talking to investors, have support from their advisers—they are in a position to execute their plans piece by piece. They know what they can base their financial assumptions on and which revenue model will allow them to grow to the volume they want. They can be an option for the huge number of college graduates coming out every year in the US, and then eventually abroad.

So what's the entire picture like, five years from now?

'One, we're definitely going to change our name, and rebrand. What we really have here is a new business emerging out of the old one. It will evolve—like a snake sheds its skin and becomes a better version of itself than before! We are really growing that way.'

A fine way to put it!

'Essentially, the reason we need to do these tests is because the market is going to tell us exactly how the future looks.'

The company later did reform itself. From TerraShift, it became ReWork and has really established itself the way Nat had predicted.

'Also, you asked five years from now, but the answer I really want to give is where we see ourselves in twenty years' time. By twenty years from now, whatever we have done will have fundamentally affected the structure of how people are employed. It will change the view of what it means to have a job. We want to make it so that the norm is not people losing their idealisms in their early twenties and compromising by falling into a day-to-day job that doesn't inspire them.'

> 'We are going to find a way to have vast numbers of people engaged in work that really fires them up.'

The vision itself is inspiring!

'Part of it has to do with us playing a role in supporting the impact in economy, social enterprises, et cetera, and helping these businesses grow; they can hire more people, figure the impact and get more investment. We want to have a new kind of company, where people can come and do a variety of projects—not just one job. They can work for a couple years, without having to worry about money, and also be focused on what their purpose and passion lie in.'

Nat feels that, in our society, we are missing a step in between going to college and having a career. People think that going to college is enough, but colleges do not do a very good job of helping people understand and align themselves with what they really want to do *and* equip themselves to do it.

It's usually one of the two:

Graduates from colleges may have skills but not know what they want to do with them.

Or, they graduate finally knowing what they want to do but having studied something different altogether!

ReWork is like a viable alternative to graduate schools, a different way of looking at higher education and what happens after college.

Right now, what is the biggest challenge they are facing?

'Luckily, there is nothing really stopping us. We are flowing forward in time and overcoming all individual obstacles. The biggest challenge had been the rebranding, but that has already been taken care of. ReWork is doing well. We are concentrating on having our language and communication right so that everybody else can understand our business and how to interact with it!'

That process is already on its way and has started happening at the Unreasonable Institute.

So, to conclude the interview, we ask Nat to sum up his mantra for us.

'Man, that is a tough one!' Nat laughs. Upon giving it a thought, he says, 'What we are taught is to make presentations, speak aloud and summon people to our cause, but what I prefer is to do things first and then later talk about them. So I never want to talk a lot about what we want to do or what we will do. I'm someone who first does things and then talks about it.'

'Something that describes me, something I have always believed in and followed is: speak little, do much.'

Of course, as we did see, the company first took their idea from a thought, to a proven concept and only after they had something solid, they approached the Unreasonable Institute. So, Nat turns out true to his word.

That is something we could all learn from him. Making plans and having a good vision is nothing if not teamed with execution because theoretical concepts are honestly nothing like what things can eventually turn out to be practically.

ReWork is working fervently and reaching its vision, one step at a time. Nat and his team have a promising future to look ahead to, for which they are working very hard.

And we think they are doing a great job!

It's all in an idea, and the willpower to implement it. Everything starts from an idea. It's how the idea is taken forward that really decides what becomes of it—it can be forgotten, left untouched forever, or it may be implemented and turn out to be powerful enough to change the entire perspective of the world.

> After all, it is not just the idea itself, but the people who believe in it and implement it that matter.

Nat and the entire team at ReWork are dedicated to their vision and have full confidence in their abilities. As it has always been with them—as long as they are true to their purpose, everything will fall into place. It's not like there won't be obstacles. There will be; there always are. There are risks involved, yes, but more than anything, ReWork finds the risk taking to be fun! They are confident about taking up the obstacles and barriers that come on the way one by one and weave their way through them—and come out a more powerful team. Like always.

## What's New?

In 2011, TerraShift evolved into ReWork. Since then it has moved from four full-time to five full-time and five part-time employees, took on clients like Acumen, Reasoning Mind and Meetup.com, and evolved into an innovative search firm serving mission-driven organizations across the US and abroad. ReWork helps hiring managers find and hire talented people by connecting them to members of its national talent pool, which is full of professionals who are excellent at what they do and want their careers to have lasting impact.

# 4

# NEVER LET OPPORTUNITIES PASS YOU BY

JENNIFER GUINTU

Jennifer Guintu graduated summa cum laude from the University of Notre Dame and earned a bachelor's degree in political science and Spanish. She received a Fulbright grant to complete an international MBA in Madrid, Spain, and it was there that her team created the business plan for Prospéritas. Later she moved to Colombia to launch Prospéritas Microfinanzas. The company dealt with empowering micro-entrepreneurs by providing economic resources and business-development services. Prospéritas aimed to provide a platform of services for micro-entrepreneurs starting with credit and basic business training to strengthen the use of the loan. The purpose of microcredit is not just to invest in microbusinesses but rather to empower micro-entrepreneurs.

After her adventures working in Colombia and in microfinance, Jennifer left Bogotá and currently lives in Spain, where she teaches English to Spaniards and prepares professionals to work in a more global market.

BORN AND raised in Southern California, Jennifer Guintu grew up in a Filipino household as both her parents had immigrated to California from the Philippines to the United States in the 1970s. Her mother worked as a medical technician. Her father is in sales—jumping from job to job, selling anything from vacuums to vitamins, right now dealing with real estate, specifically memorial property, and here's the interesting bit: on the weekends, he is a DJ.

'He definitely has a work–life balance. Music is what makes him happy. He plays at weddings, birthdays and corporate events, so, he's happy!'

Her parents were the first to move to the US in their respective families and, later, their extended families started to migrate to California too. Jennifer considers herself lucky to have grown up with her whole family around—uncles, aunts and cousins. She has been very close to both sides of her family and has become used to parties every weekend—family gatherings and barbeques.

'When I was growing up, there were a lot of kids my age in the neighbourhood and we used to play on the streets. I was able to grow up in a cul-de-sac so we could play without caring about cars and traffic. One of my neighbours had a tree house . . . so, overall, it was a very typical, sheltered environment growing up.'

When she was younger, did she want to be something?

Without stopping for a second to think or even breathe, Jennifer exclaims, 'Indiana Jones. The female version!'

She wanted to travel the world to make big discoveries and solve mysteries. She has been fascinated by the intersections of history and culture and travelling really struck a note with her. So, Indiana Jones was the reasonable (or should we say *unreasonable*?) answer to that!

She attended private schools, St Judes from kindergarten to eighth grade and then she joined an all-girls Catholic high school called La Reina High School. She went to a Catholic college—the University of Notre Dame. She has had a Catholic orientation all her life. Her parents put great value on education, for which she is grateful. Her parents worked very hard and sacrificed a lot for the family.

'My mom, at one point, took up two full-time jobs, trying to keep all of us in school.'

Jennifer has three siblings, an elder brother James, who is six years older to Jennifer. An elder sister Judy, who is four years older, and a younger brother Joseph, who is two years younger to Jennifer.

She always had a fascination with history when she was in high school. She was in the Model United Nations Club, founder of the Spanish Club, a part of Amnesty International—so she tried a little bit of everything in school. She did a bunch of stuff—some for cultural perspective and some for international.

'When I was seventeen, they pitched a summer programme in Mexico. It was a four-week programme, and because I would get college credit from it, my parents were sold on the idea! And when I went there, I had an eye-opening experience.'

The opportunity to participate in that exchange programme in Mexico when she was in high school opened her eyes and she realized that she had been living in a bubble, which is Southern California. Just the conversations taught her a lot and changed her perspective.

Her professor in Mexico once said to her, about Southern California, 'Just because we want to move there does not mean we want to be like the people there.' It was a simple statement, but it struck Jennifer.

'When we were there, we climbed a mountain in Tepotzlán. The ancients say that there is a source of energy there. When I reached the top, maybe it was the blood rushing to my head, but I definitely felt the source of energy. I had one of those moments, where I felt a connection with the environment. And that's when I realized that, wow, I have the travel bug!'

She felt amazing.

'Standing on the top of the Tepozteco mountain, I thought, "There's so much more to see, feel and do." That was my Indiana Jones experience!'

Back in school, when she was in the seventh grade, she was the commissioner of safety and ecology. She got to do the fire drills and earthquake drills. In eighth grade, she was the student body president. In high school, she was always active in extracurricular activities and she graduated as the high school salutatorian.

When she finished school, she did not have a clear idea of what she wanted to do next. The experience in Mexico shaped her decision to eventually choose government and international relations. She went to the Midwest again because she wanted to 'leave the bubble' and took it as a chance to meet other people from her country. Since the US is so huge, she decided to explore it. Also, the college seemed like a good place to be for an eighteen- to twenty-two-year-old.

'I definitely loved my university. The weather—not so much! I chose government and international relations. I had a mentor, Adela Penagos, a Spanish professor, hailing from Mexico and it was good to get a perspective from her.'

When, in her freshman year, Jennifer decided to apply to go to Mexico, her mentor suggested she choose Spain instead. Adela thought that travelling Europe at the age of eighteen would be perfect for Jennifer. Jennifer agreed, and was in the process of applying to Spain, when again her mentor asked her to go for a year! One out of four years of graduation spent abroad seemed like a good plan. So Jennifer went to Spain as a sophomore in college, for a year.

'Adela said to me, "By the time the semester is over, you'll feel that you've just started and got comfortable in this new city. You don't want to go home just after three or four months." So, taking her advice, I spent my entire sophomore year in Spain.'

When she was there, she did an internship in an office for the European Union. She lived in Toledo, Spain, and experienced a total environmental shift. Back in Southern

California, people used to think that she was a Filipino, judging from her characteristics and facial features. But in Spain, people treated her as an American, since all her traits were like an American, as she was born and raised in the US. The identity shift gave Jennifer a better perspective on American culture.

'Once, during my internship, talking about the European Union, the guy I was working with said, "When the US sneezes, Europe catches a cold." I started to open my eyes to what my identity as an American is and what being an American means politically. I had grown up in a very safe and sheltered environment.'

Another interesting thing happened in Jennifer's sophomore year—she met her current fiancé. He was invited to sing at the welcome party, and that's where they met. He was a student at the university Jennifer was attending. He was a part of a traditional group called La Tuna which every university there has. The group dressed up in medieval clothes and sang songs. They are known for serenading women.

Jennifer's Spanish language classes came in handy!

'Alejandro is Spanish, and dating him was absolutely fabulous, because I was forced to speak in Spanish, all the time. Usually, you go to Spain for a student exchange programme and you end up travelling a lot and seeing a lot of Spanish culture, but you don't get to speak Spanish so much, since you're stuck with American friends. With Alejandro, his friends and family, I got a special insight into Spanish culture.'

They were together in Spain for ten months, after which Jennifer got back to the US and they decided to go for a long-distance relationship. They saw each other during summers or

Christmas holidays. Jennifer's three remaining years at Notre Dame were memorable. She was active in extracurricular activities, spent time with her friends, concentrated on her academic progress and kept the relationship with Alejandro sailing—all at once.

'I had a lot of fun at Notre Dame. I was also very active in extracurricular activities, so I got to spend time with my girlfriends, was able to focus on my studies and, since Alejandro was abroad, I didn't feel like I was neglecting my boyfriend!'

Very clever! Nice little arrangement she'd got there!

'I don't think I missed out on anything. I did it all.'

She had graduated from high school with college credit, which gave her some flexibility later in college. By the time she graduated from college, her major had changed to political science. She graduated with a double major in political science and Spanish and a minor in European studies. She thought about applying to the Department of State as the concept of travelling and living in other cultures has been appealing to her.

'I graduated in 2003, which was just a year and a half after 9/11. People told me that if I work at the Department of State, I'd start at the bottom, which means I could be sent to really dangerous countries. So I decided I did not want to be there.'

'Then, out of the blue, I thought I wanted to join law school. I told my mentor that and she asked me why. I said, "International law sounds cool!" And she asked me if I even knew what international law is!'

Her mentor, Adela, advised her not to go for law, just as a default option, not knowing what she really wanted to do.

Jennifer did not join a law school and went back to California, still undecided.

A job opportunity came up through a contact to work at Deutsche Bank and Jennifer took it. She had not been exposed to the corporate world and wanted the experience. She joined the bank as a portfolio accounting analyst. The environment was very dynamic, with lots of young people on the team.

At the bank, she was in charge of five or six different portfolios and her job was to monitor cash flow, execute trades, close accounts on a daily basis and manage portfolio compliance tests.

Not bad for a twenty-two-year-old!

After two years of working there, she got more responsibilities. She had to be there at closings, do the bond issuance process and other such tasks that needed her to interact with others, like lawyers, rating agencies, auditors, portfolio managers and investors. She observed the things that happen behind the scenes with different actors in finance.

The company treated Jennifer well and she was very fond of the corporate culture. She worked long hours, but did not mind that at such a young age. At twenty-four, she had a lot of energy and was very enthusiastic about her work.

'After a while, I thought, "I'm doing all this stuff, and I know how to do it, but I don't know why." I did not understand the finance behind it. And I was not making any decisions; I was executing them. I needed more.'

She was twenty-six by then, and had recently bought a condo in Long Beach with her brother. Instead of renting, they had decided to put in some money and buy a place together. So Jennifer had a condo, had bought a new car, had a decent salary—but that was not enough.

> 'Had I been forty-six, it would have been the perfect scenario. I would have just settled down. But I was just twenty-six. And I realized—there has to be more to this; this cannot be it.'

How did the realization strike—was there a day when this occurred or was it a gradual development?

'Over time, the novelty of jobs wears off. I started looking at MBA programmes and my brother suggested that I go for a Fulbright to Spain. I looked into it and found a programme for a one-year MBA in Madrid at the business school and the Fulbright would pay for the full tuition and allow a monthly stipend. More than that, I thought it was perfect because Alejandro was in Spain and Madrid is not very far from Toledo.'

She applied for that and also to the University of California, Los Angeles (UCLA). She got into both, but the course UCLA offered was three years long, where she had to work full-time and study part-time.

'I decided it was better to do a paid one-year MBA, which would be paid for, and *not* have to work full-time . . . *and* be in Spain! I was very, very lucky.'

But around that time, in March of 2007, her younger brother—Joseph—met an unfortunate accident. He was out surfing, when he complained of back pain, which his instructor brushed away as nothing important. Later, when he got back to his hotel, he went to see his hotel doctor, who rushed him to the hospital emergency room. A few hours later, Joseph was paralysed from the waist down.

'It's easier for us to understand things if we know why. We didn't know why this happened to Joseph—he didn't hit a rock, the waves didn't hit him in a certain way, so we didn't know how he could go from walking to not walking in a matter of hours, with no impact on the spinal cord.'

It turned out that the way he was surfing cut off the blood supply to his spine. They flew him from Hawaii to Denver, where he was admitted into a spinal-cord rehabilitation centre called Craig Hospital. The doctors there were confused, since Joseph had a very rare condition called surfer's myelopathy.

'A lot of doctors hadn't even heard of it before. It happens to first-time surfers. The odds of getting surfer's myelopathy are very, very low—it's like winning the lottery.'

> 'Life can change in a second. You have to take advantage of opportunities, but also enjoy every moment.'

'You see different levels of injury in Craig Hospital. Joseph's roommate was a sixteen-year-old who had been in a car accident.

And after seeing Joseph and all the patients around him, it struck me that everything can change completely in one moment.'

But Jennifer's brother was a strong man. His physiotherapist claimed that he had the best attitude around the hospital. They had never seen anyone with so much strength, someone who was so positive in a context that was so challenging.

Joseph is still in a wheelchair, four years later. But he hasn't stopped fighting. He goes to the gym, senses feeling in his legs, he has muscle strength and sometimes he can push an exercise bike with his legs. The progress is slow, but he has not given up. He has returned to work, at Deloitte. He can function independently and is an inspiration to Jennifer.

So, she was about to go to Spain, when her brother's accident happened. What changed for her, at that point?

'I almost stayed. We were close and I could not leave him. But Joseph told me to go. He said, "I have to move on and so do you." And I did. Even in that dark time, he was the one with strength.'

> 'Things aren't always as bad as you think they are. Or if they really are bad, then you have to find ways to overcome them and move on.'

Joseph and his wife started a foundation to create awareness about his condition. Part of the mission is to teach surf instructors about the risks of pushing someone to surf, past a limit.

On his insistence, Jennifer went to Spain. The course was a one-year intensive, accelerated MBA programme. There were 280 students in her class, out of which 80 per cent were from outside of Spain, because of which they became a very close and tight family.

Jennifer became friends with Marcela Torres, who had worked on a microfinance pilot project in Columbia, before coming to Madrid. They were randomly placed in a group together to work on a project for their entrepreneurship class. They worked on the same pilot project Marcella was involved in earlier. By working on that project, Jennifer realized the potential microfinance had and its large impact.

'It clicked. I thought, "Here's a possibility to do something sustainable as a business and create a large impact at the same time." It made sense.'

They created a team and worked on that project. They participated in a competition called Venture Lab and submitted their business plan. They won the competition, which came with access to €30,000 at zero per cent interest rate over five years. Jennifer and Marcela decided to launch the company.

'By that time, my MBA was completed. And I thought, "When am I going to get such an opportunity again?" I had a chance to start my own business, to live in a foreign country that is completely different to the other foreign countries I had lived in and to create a large impact for deserving people.'

All this while, not once did Jennifer think of joining a multinational company and making big bucks through that. She did not look for any of it. For her, working on this microfinance company had only upside; she did not turn to look at what she was forgoing by going through with her venture.

> 'This was my opportunity to change the world. The way I saw it I had no other option but to take it.'

After her MBA, Jennifer went back to California to touch base with her family. She moved to Columbia in June of 2009. The idea was to reach a hundred clients in six months, from the money they won in that competition and their own money. And through that process, refine their operations. This way, they could gain confidence by the time it was time to pitch to investors.

'It's important that when we reach the investors, we can say, "We have tried this and this is how it works, and these are the results." And of course, you are able to negotiate a larger share in your company, when your pilot plan has been successful.'

They set up an office in Bogotá and hired a lawyer to take care of the contracts. They spent the first two months going through logistics, reading the contracts and officially incorporating the company.

Their first employee was their first client from the pilot project, who was Marcela's housekeeper—Dalila Dalila. One day, Marcela had asked Dalila if she had a dream, to which Dalila had replied that she would love to have her own hot dog stand! Marcela lent $125 to her for the hot dog stand and in two months Dalila doubled her income.

'We can teach hard skills, but teaching soft skills is very difficult. Dalila was our analyst—she found clients, helped them fill out application forms, and got back to us after doing the background checks on every client.'

For Jennifer's company—Prospéritas Microfinanzas—scaling up has been a problem and they have not grown as fast as they would have liked to. Funding is the main issue, like with every other growing company.

'Some businesses are able to start off with a little money and provide services. Our service is lending money, so we need a lot of it.' Jennifer laughs. 'We don't know how to test our growth model without money—that is the most frustrating part.'

(Jennifer's fiancé, Alejandro, moved to Columbia six months after she did and they have been living together since. He was doing a master's in history, on a full scholarship and a stipend.)

## What's New?

Her venture had still been in the beginning stages when she applied to the Unreasonable Institute and was selected. Since then, a lot has changed and Prospéritas Microfinanzas has developed significantly.

Jennifer says that microfinance on the books is beautiful, but when she actually went on the ground, it was not that easy. There are things about the industry that Jennifer does not agree with—some lending practices and issues of transparency, which she isn't fond of.

'What I have learnt about Columbia is that you have to

earn the trust. It has a violent history and there is a lot of corruption and disparity. All these elements combined—it's not a community that easily trusts others. It's a community that is very open and hospitable and has treated me well. But when it's about business transactions, they are not going to trust me off the bat.'

It was very different from the city she had grown up in, which was trusting and had the concept of 'innocent till proven guilty'. Setting up their new business there, without having an established brand or name recognition and not coming across as a 'loan shark' or charity was a fight.

What does her average day look like today?

'I wake up, go into the office, look at payments that we received from the day before, match them to expected payments, generate a report of who we need to call to let them know that we are aware of the late payment and find out why that happened by communicating with the client. We prepare the list one day before the credit analyst needs to visit the clients. Mostly—it depends—on any given day, I can be an errand messenger or I can be the president!'

The urgent social need that Prospéritas is addressing is to provide a chance to deserving candidates to start their own businesses. Almost 50 per cent of the Colombian population lives in poverty. Opportunities for a stable income and employment are scarce, therefore creating a cycle of poverty where access to tools for economic success (education, health services, et cetera) is limited. Much of the labour force works in the informal sector. This sector is full of creative, resourceful and hard-working Colombians. With limited access to credit at just interest rates and with insufficient education and training, most microbusinesses in the informal economy are unsustainable. Opportunities for credit in the informal sector lie with local usurers who charge abusive monthly interest rates of 20 per cent. And 54 lakh Colombian microenterprises are in need of just credit. Microfinance institutes (MFIs) are only able to meet 25 per cent of the market need.

'We have seen first-hand that microcredit, under responsible lending methodologies, works to slowly improve the quality of life of our clients.'

How has she found the experience so far?

'It's been an amazing experience. People in Columbia, unfortunately, have a negative stereotype: drugs, violence, the paramilitaries, et cetera. But in my time there, I have come to respect this place. It's nothing like what people think it is.'

To summarize it all, we ask Jennifer to tell us what threads together everything she has done. What has been her personal philosophy through all of this?

'It's a big question. I have been pondering over it too, for some time. It's important to take a step back and think things through,' Jennifer says. 'It's kind of like when in college, you are an undergrad and you wonder what you want to major in!'

She thinks it over for a while, before quoting Socrates, 'I only know that I know nothing.'

'I've spent my life learning. I learn from people, different cultures. Sometimes, I take a step back from being a manager and learn how to be a better manager—see other models, find out other ways of approaching a situation.'

'Life has so many surprises. The minute I think I know something, somebody or something surprises me and says, "Not what you thought!"'

Sometimes you think you know something and, later, it turns out to be just the tip of an iceberg. That's what reminds us to be humble and modest. And that is how we keep on learning and growing.

After going through this experience, Jennifer can see herself as a serial entrepreneur. In the process of going to college, followed by a job, an MBA and establishing a new business, she has learnt a lot of things and grown a lot. And, of course, still keeps growing! The attitude of never thinking you know enough and the will to learn more and more certainly takes you places.

'I have grown so much, learnt so much about myself and I'm still learning a lot.'

If she had been asked before she had done her MBA, she would have said that she has low risk tolerance and that she preferred stability and security. But her experience has given her confidence and belief in her ability to be an entrepreneur.

'I can see myself as a serial entrepreneur, who keeps doing new stuff. And hopefully with every new venture or project, I grow wiser and smarter. But always learning.'

# 5

# CREATING IMPACT

Ties Kroezen is the managing director of NICE International, which is an innovative and sustainable social venture that has developed the NICE Concept: overcoming barriers to access of energy and the Internet in developing countries. NICE centres provide technology solutions for education, work and business.

Ties Kroezen joined NICE in 2008, building it from a pilot project into a profitable business with seven locations in the Gambia. His ambition is to make NICE the 'McDonald's of Africa'. However, instead of selling burgers, the hundreds of NICE centres will sell information and communications technology (ICT)–based development services to local people.

Their aim is to distribute development products and services in base-of-the-pyramid markets through a network of solar-powered ICT centres operated by local entrepreneurs on a franchise basis.

TIES' BACKGROUND is a very interesting story in itself. His father, Ties Sr, belongs to a large family of over twenty, from a village in the Netherlands, known as Beesd. From amongst twenty children that his parents had, Ties Sr was the nineteenth in number and the first to go to college. His father was a staunch Catholic and sent Ties Sr to a seminary, since he wanted one of his children to become a priest, and Ties Sr showed the intellect for it. Ties Sr was seventeen years old, and a number of years into the priest education, when he decided to quit and go to a university to study economics. His father was furious; he was waiting for his son to become a priest and bring glory to the family. He did not talk to Ties Sr for two years, after which they reconciled their differences.

Ties' mother, on the other hand, came from a family of seventeen children, of whom she was the fourteenth born. Her father was a businessman from a town in another part of the Netherlands called Medemblik.

After getting married, Ties' parents relocated to Haarlem, Netherlands. They had four children, of whom Ties is the third born (1963). His father was an economist and his mother ran the household.

'Initially, I used to be a shy, skinny little boy. When I entered the secondary school, I became quite a troublemaker! I was sent out of class very often. I think it's safe to say I spent more time outside than inside!'

Ever since the beginning, Ties had trouble deciding what he wanted to do in the future.

In primary school, he used to have a deep interest in history. He wanted to be an archaeologist when he grew up. But the phase faded by the time he entered secondary school.

In secondary school, his biggest passion lay in rowing. He used to practise rowing for twenty hours every week, which he believes had a positive impact on his life. It gave a structure to his days and divided his time. He was not extremely good at it, but he worked hard and enjoyed it.

After secondary school, he still had no clear idea of what he wanted to do next. He decided to study business, since its broad scope would leave many options open. At eighteen, he joined University of Twente, from where he graduated in 1987 with a master's in business science.

(That was where he met his wife—Nicole. It was 1987 and she was studying textiles management, after which she joined the fashion business.)

Again, after passing out with his master's degree, Ties did not quite know what to do next.

He went for his sixteen months of mandatory military service, where he had mostly a desk job, since he had gone to a college and had a university degree.

'After that was done, I still had no idea what I wanted to do next. It's kind of like the story of my life; I never knew which direction to take. It gave me a chance to try my hand at everything that caught my fancy.'

He landed a job as a consultant at Andersen Consulting (now known as Accenture) and, before starting, he decided to travel through Brazil for three months, with a friend of his. He says, 'It was a once-in-a-lifetime chance of doing some proper travelling, before we got caught up in other things.'

It was his first time on an airplane and first experience of visiting a developing country. He met all kinds of people there, ranging from the extremely rich to the extremely poor. 'We went beyond being tourists. If you go to visit a place for a couple of weeks, you race around like an idiot, jumping from one place to another, trying to see it all. You try to make the most of your time. But when you live there for three months, increasingly, you become a part of the life there.'

They experienced getting stranded in the middle of nowhere, on a boat with the engine not working.

'One particularly interesting experience was when we went to the Amazon by a boat. This was a boat where you had to bring your own hammock. The trip to a city called Manaus was supposed to take three days. This boat was filled with hammocks, so if one person moved, everybody had to move. We became good friends with all the guys on the boat; they were mostly gold prospectors, looking to find gold in the Amazon.'

'Then one day, the engine of the boat broke down, somewhere in the middle of nowhere. Along the river, we caught sight of a small village. We spent two days in that village, before they could send another boat to come and pick us up. And that was fantastic—it was a village that has never seen white people before and we were treated like celebrities!'

After getting back, Ties joined Andersen. He was given a

pile of thick books to complete in the span of three weeks, after which he was sent to Chicago for a boot camp with five or six new recruits.

This was his first real job. Earlier, he had been paid a small salary in the army, and, in college, he used to assist a professor, for which he earned an income, but this was the first full-time, proper job.

In Chicago, they were picked up by a stretch limousine to be taken from the airport to the Andersen campus. In the training centre, they were amongst all the recruits from all over the world. They had to work very hard—from 8 a.m. to 10 p.m. The training set the culture of the company into the new recruits. They were there for three weeks, before coming back and joining work.

He worked at Andersen for six years—moving from junior consultant to senior consultant to engagement manager. Ties liked working there—the company promised to deliver high-quality work before strict deadlines, so they worked very hard. He worked in the private sector of the company (they also had a government sector).

His first engagement manager was a good mentor to him. After four years, Ties was given a chance to go to London for a year to work on an international showcase project for Andersen called Smart Store Europe. He went there with his girlfriend Nicole (who is now his wife) and lived downtown, where the rent was more than his salary, but, luckily, the company took care of that.

There was a team of about twenty to twenty-five consultants from all over Europe, and some from the US, working on this project. For Andersen, this project was basically a marketing tool.

'It was very inspiring. As a young man, you do not get many such chances to work with an international team and do workshops with the management of some of the most successful companies in Europe.'

After getting back to the Netherlands, Ties took the post of a consumer products specialist, which he earned by being on that project in the UK. But back in the Netherlands, his job was not as challenging or interesting as the one year in the UK had been. So he decided to switch to a business strategy consulting firm, where he could do the kind of work he wanted to do.

Ties joined a small consulting firm—Robert Pino & Company—which had just about ten employees. It was a very entrepreneurial company, small, but delivering top-quality work. Their focus was mainly the consumer market, so they worked with companies such as Unilever, Heineken and the like. Ties was not working harder than he did at Accenture, but he was the second-most experienced employee there, after the owner. At Accenture, he had mostly dealt with delivery, but here, he got more involved in sales, along with internal management and delivery.

'I had a good time there, but, after a couple of years, I was still the most experienced person there. I had learnt a lot from the owner, but after the time I had spent there and in Andersen, I had seen all the tricks, and there was no surprise. Also, there wasn't a possibility of becoming a partner, because the man I was working for was the sole owner of the business and wanted to grow it and sell it, which he later did. So, I decided to move on.'

Ties moved to yet another consulting firm—Nolan, Norton & Co. (NNC). NNC was a part of KPMG at that time. (KPMG is one of the largest professional-services companies in the world and one of the Big Four auditors, along with Deloitte, Ernst & Young and PricewaterhouseCoopers.) Though they were part of KPMG, they were a separate unit, and taken alone, they were a midsized consulting firm.

The company's focus was the edge between business and ICT strategies, where Ties applied his ICT background from Accenture. Another thing Ties liked about them was that they had a strong link with the academic world—they had their own research institute and two employees who were part-time professors at a university. The academic link assured that there were new ideas, concepts and models coming forward all the time.

Ties worked there for five years, in the consumer-products and HR-services departments. By then, he was forty, and had been a consultant for fifteen years.

'That was when I realized that I loved this field and I could do consulting for the next twenty or twenty-five years. Becoming a partner in Nolan, Norton & Co. was a prospect, but I decided to extend my horizon outside the consulting industry.'

Ties had a curiosity to see the world. Before they had children, he used to travel to developing countries with his wife, every year. They travelled to India, Indonesia, South America—always backpacking to new lands.

One day, Ties came across an advertisement in the newspaper from SNV, which is a Dutch development organization. (Ties' brother had done development work for many years after his graduation, in places like Kenya and Ecuador, for SNV. So, Ties knew about SNV's work, and it really appealed to him.) In the ad that SNV had put in the paper, they were specifically looking for people who were not from the developing sector. They were looking for someone to become a country director for them.

'I saw the ad and I thought, "That's me; that's the kind of job I would like to do." Part of the appeal was going to an entirely new country, especially a developing country, and living your life in a completely different way from how you used to. Also, the idea that with my experience I could really contribute to private sector development work.'

Ties was not from the developing sector, so he thought himself to be the perfect candidate. Keeping that thought in mind, he applied. Apparently, they had a lot of applications. Ties was picked based on his letter, and had a telephonic interview, after which Ties did not hear from them for over three weeks. In his head, he was trying to paint a picture of what would happen if he got the job—what he would do with his family, his house, and other such practical questions. He did not know which country he would be sent to, since SNV was looking for several country heads for different developing countries at a time. But he was excited about the prospect.

'The job was perfect—a balanced mix of ideals and adventure.'

But he did not hear from them for many more weeks. One day, he gave them a call and found out that he was not selected for the job. Having thought about working there for so long, the idea had stuck in his head, and he was very disappointed about the company's decision of not hiring him. He started looking for more job options in the same field of work.

'That was very frustrating. For a total of two years, I sent out a number of applications to different organizations and, consistently, I was never even invited for an interview. My applications got rejected right away. I tried contacting the HR department of SNV for an open interview to at least give me a fair chance. I tried to pull strings through my brother, but none of it worked. I had been applying for different vacancies for almost two years, and was on the verge of giving up. It was not as if I was not qualified. I had some big names in my CV and was offering my services, but no one spared me a look.'

Just when Ties was about to give up on the whole idea, he got a call for an interview from ICCO, which is a Dutch development agency. They were looking for someone to start up a social business in Ghana. He was picked for the job and he decided to move to Ghana with his family. His wife had quit her work in the textile industry and was studying to become a primary school teacher. She was okay with shifting to a new place.

Ties faced a severe salary cut when he quit his job at Nolan, Norton & Co. He was paid a good sum, as compared to the local standard in Ghana, but compared with his salary at NNC it was significantly less. But he really had his heart set on doing something meaningful, something that left an impact on people's lives.

'I handed in my nice Audi company car, gave up my lifestyle and house and moved with my family to Ghana. It was quite a step, to put it mildly.' But his heart really knew what it wanted.

> 'I used to ask myself, when I'm dead would I want "he has consulted many companies" written on my gravestone? Or would it be better if "he had improved the lives of many people" was carved there instead?'

It was 2004 and Ties went to Ghana alone, to find a place and settle down, make sure there was furniture and make other such arrangements before the family followed, by the end of the year. His kids were aged six and four at the time, and it was a convenient time for them to shift, without being too worried about the children's health, since they were no longer babies, or about their education, since they were still just in primary school.

'We took the gamble. And I had a fantastic time—at work and at home. At home, it was like starting all over again. We found the four of us together, in a faraway country, where we hardly knew anybody and didn't know how things worked—so it did feel like starting all over again. We got into a rhythm in our day-to-day life, but starting again in a completely different environment is actually an amazing experience.'

The project that Ties was recruited for dealt with connecting cotton farmers to the spinning and weaving mills—their company had to act as an intermediary. That wing of the project was Ties' responsibility. The other leg of the project was to train the same farmers, to help them organize themselves into groups to then become cooperatives that would be shareholders in the intermediate company (Savanna Farmers Marketing Company or SFMC) that they were setting up.

When they explored the idea more, they realized that it was a very good plan, but not for cotton. There were legal constraints, there was the fact that cotton production requires a huge quantity of pesticides, which they did not approve of and several other factors that had initially been overlooked.

They decided to replace cotton with other crops. They analysed several other crops and picked three—sorghum, soybean and groundnuts. It was January, and they had to set up the company and organize operations in four months' time to be prepared by the start of the farming season (May–June) that same year.

'We had an extremely tight schedule, because we had to set up a company which did not exist at the time. We had to get the company registered, get funding, set up accounts, prepare the business model, secure a market with a buyer and then go out to the farmers and tell them they could produce for the market in question.'

They found three buyers—two local and one international—and then went to the farmers to inform them about the project and prep them to sign contracts to work with the company. The interest was overwhelming—they ended up with 3000 farmers in the first year, in ten different districts in northern Ghana.

The team worked closely together to find buyers, educate farmers and set up the company. All they needed next was funding. They looked for funding, but venture capital did not exist and banks did not show any interest, since they were not just a start-up but a start-up in agriculture. They went to ICCO, which provided a grant to a local NGO in Ghana, which in turn paid it to SFMC as equity capital, thus becoming a shareholder in the company.

That's how they started in 2005. Harvesting was in August–September, so throughout the summer they trained the farmers. Never once did Ties regret his decision of quitting his consulting career and as he puts it, 'I was having lots of fun!'

It was harvest time and the volume of sorghum and soybean was as expected, but it was not the same with groundnuts. With groundnuts, the volumes were not coming at all. They learnt that that was because the market price had gone above their price. Initially, they had gone in with a fixed price, to provide security to the farmers. In the contract, a very good price was stated—and that was the price the farmers would receive from the company in harvest season upon delivering the produce. The price that seemed like a very good price to the farmers while signing the contract was lower than the market price later, since the latter had gone up on account of the production of groundnuts being very low in that area in that particular farming season.

'The farmers, who had taken our credit for the seed and ploughing, sold their produce to other buyers. Without telling us, of course. They were telling us all kinds of stories and excuses for not delivering—like their farm had caught fire.

They would harvest, sell the produce and then set whatever was remaining of the farm on fire to make their story credible.'

Due to the low volume of groundnuts they received, they faced three problems. First, they could not supply to their buyers as promised and the buyers got furious and started talking about claims and whatnot. Second, the farmers who had taken up credit from the company could not pay back the money—since the deal was that they would pay back *through* their produce, which they had sold to someone else. The third was, to cover their overheads, they needed volume to make some margin—since if the volume is not there, you don't get your coverage for overheads.

They learnt a lot of things from that first season and, from the next, they made changes in the business model so that these mistakes were not repeated. They stopped having completely fixed rates and made the contracts flexible instead. In the second year, they had around 4000 to 5000 farmers, whom they got in touch with through the NGO they were working with. Sometimes, Ties had to be the one talking to the farmers, convincing them and bringing them in.

> 'That was one of the fun parts of my job. One moment, I could be talking to Guinness headquarters, and the next, sitting under a mango tree with a group of illiterate farmers, talking about their farms.'

Ties always felt as if it was his job to bring the two worlds together because their company was positioned in between.

In the second year, things went much better and they started making a profit. In Ties' third and last year on the project, they looked for someone to replace him after he left the next year, since his contract with them was for three years only. The lady whom they brought in worked with the team for the third year. She was very efficient and handled the business well, so Ties saw no reason to extend his contract.

'I built up a business from nothing in Africa, so that gave me a lot of useful lessons with which I decided to move on.'

Ties was open to doing another stint in a developing country and his wife was up for it too, but then, he was asked to join two ICCO managers who were starting up a new organization—FairMatch Support. This project was based in the Netherlands, so they went back. It was the summer of 2007 when Ties joined them as one of the three founders. FairMatch Support tried to link farmers in developing countries to the market in Europe for sustainable products like fair trade and organic products. It worked more or less along the same lines as the Ghana project.

ICCO funded the operation and Ties handled the finance and project development. But he did not have good chemistry with the team he was working with—the other two founders of FairMatch Support. They had a disagreement in terms of where they wanted to see the company go. Ties could see he could not work there for much longer.

So, what next?

The next big question he faced was: developing or consultancy? He had to decide whether he wanted to do something in consultancy again, or continue his career in social entrepreneurship. Once again unsure, he applied for both, at several places.

He soon had four offers—two from consulting, two from social enterprises. One of the offers from the developing sector was from NICE International, which he decided to take, despite a consulting offer paying him three times the salary!

'The offer from NICE was very challenging. NICE was a venture of Econcern, which was a very successful, very fast-growing renewable energy company. They were based in the Netherlands, but were working all over the world, in solar energy, wind energy and the like.'

When Ties joined NICE, it had been running for two years. The company was set up by a young enthusiastic staff of Econcern. Ties replaced him as the manager with the task of developing NICE to profitability and scaling it up.

The company had a history behind it—when an executive from the Dutch energy industry, Paul van Son, went to the Gambia for a leadership programme in the year 2003, he saw that most villages did not have a proper supply of electricity. So upon coming back to the Netherlands, he planned to set up a foundation to develop business solutions for access to energy and other infrastructures in the off-grid areas. In 2004, Energy4All Foundation was established, with one of the founders being the chairman of Econcern. The initial idea was to set up a sea container with solar panels on top, which they later found was not feasible. They decided to approach the question from the demand side and started analysing what people would need the electricity for. They decided to develop a concept that would combine solar energy with IT and the

Internet, thereby giving people access to not only energy but also to the Internet. In 2006, Econcern decided to invest in a first pilot for this concept. In 2007, NICE Gambia set up the first pilot NICE centres in Brikama and Wellingara.

NICE International was not in a very good shape when Ties joined as the managing director. Ties started working on improving the profitability of the existing two NICE centres. Six months after he joined NICE, Econcern went bankrupt. The future of NICE looked very bleak, since Econcern was their only shareholder and funder.

Ties still saw a future for NICE, so he decided to look for another source of funding. He found two—one was Essent (the same company where Paul van Son worked before setting up the Energy4All Foundation) and the other was Rabobank, which is a leading Dutch bank. They did not want to be shareholders yet, but agreed to fund NICE, transferring the shares to Energy4All Foundation. They would then give grants to Energy4All, which could then be used to finance the business.

'I shifted my office to Rabobank, and with the money they put in, we could set up four more NICE centres in 2009 and 2010. When I started, the revenues were €1000 to €1500 a month per centre. But in about six to eight months, we reached the break-even point and the revenue was like €2000 to €2500 a month per centre.'

What's a typical NICE centre like?

'It's roughly the size of two school classes. It has a solar energy system on the roof. There's a reception area inside and one or two computer rooms, where there are a number of computers connected to the Internet and a printer and scanner. Most NICE centres have a cinema—which has a big TV screen where people can watch TV, but it is also connected to a computer, so we can display images. It also has a DVD player. That's essentially what a NICE centre looks like.'

They had a subsidy from the government, for the expansion of NICE, for going from two to seven centres in the Gambia. In subsidies, they do not pay the money up front; they pay it afterwards. The subsidy was waiting for them, but they had to bring the results first, in order to get it. But again, in order to get results, they needed to find money to buy the equipment. They got that money from the two funders.

In the spring of 2010, the money they had ran out, as predicted. That was their second crisis—they had no more money to continue. Once more, NICE was about to die. Rabobank agreed to provide funding till the end of the year and the CSR director of Rabobank suggested making a joint visit to their subsidiary banks in Africa to discuss with management and find out whether they thought there could be synergy between their business and NICE. So that's what they did. The new money would allow them to continue the business and expand.

By the end of the year, the money ran out again and, this time round, there was nobody to rescue it.

'We decided to wrap up the mother company in the Netherlands. It was September 2010, and we wanted to close the company in a neat way, completing all the obligations by the end of the year. The employees would get a chance to look for new jobs, too, in that time.'

Meanwhile, the company in the Gambia was doing well. It had five centres and two more were almost ready to be set up. Ties, along with some business partners, offered to buy the company in the Gambia because chances were that it would collapse, too, when the company in the Netherlands shut down. Ties was negotiating with the shareholders to get the shares in the Gambia company.

'The plan was to shut the company in the Netherlands on the last day of December. Midway through December, I received a mail from Brussels saying, "Congratulations, your grant application has been accepted." In the beginning of 2010, we had applied to the European Union for a grant from their energy fund. We knew the application was out, but we had no idea of our chances. We were awarded a subsidy of two and a half million euros.'

The money from the grant was not very easily available. They had to provide a million euros of co-funding, which they did not have. And they knew it would take at least another six months for the money from the grant to come in. But they had to find a way—it was an opportunity that they had been waiting for, which would allow them to scale up.

'I started looking for investors. We were going through a money crunch. If we could set up the seventh centre, then we could claim the subsidy we had from the Dutch government. I urged my suppliers to be patient. We wanted to avoid bankruptcy.'

While Ties was looking for investors, Rabobank decided to cover their expenses for some months, and also offered to put in the first quarter of the million for the co-funding. They suddenly saw prospects in NICE, now that the European Union was willing to grant two and a half million euros to the company.

Ties was successful in finding three investors with serious interest in investing in NICE—Rabobank, FMO (a Dutch development bank) and Schneider Electric (a French firm which also has a fund for developing countries' energy projects). The negotiations with these investors took quite some time but, in October 2011, the contracts were signed and the EU grant was secured.

Around the same time, Ties became an Unreasonable Fellow, 2011.

The project for which the funding was provided aims to expand NICE to Tanzania and Zambia and to set up a total of fifty new NICE centres in four years' time. They are now one year into the project and things are not going as planned. Due to market changes, they were forced to modify their business concept. They are now testing a revised business concept with more focus on value-added and income-generating services. Based on the results of this test, they will decide on further expansion.

NICE addresses a social need by providing access to basic services, such as electricity and the Internet, which is a strong driver for economic growth in developing countries. The World Bank found that a 10 per cent increase in Internet access increases GDP by 1.1 to 1.4 per cent. However, access to the Internet in sub-Saharan Africa is still below 10 per cent, due to the cost of computers and connectivity and lack of electricity. The Internet can provide access to information, knowledge, networks and markets. ICT skills are demanded by many employers but not taught at most schools. ICT services can enhance rural development, increase access to and quality of education, reduce transport to main cities for basic services and play a major role in targeting vulnerable groups for poverty-alleviating projects.

NICE centres provide affordable access to energy, ICT, the Internet and development services, such as education. For companies and development organizations, NICE centres offer an efficient communication and distribution channel to the base of the pyramid. Customers have to pay for the services, enabling financial sustainability and ensuring that real needs are addressed. Using a franchise model, scaling up is a powerful thread embedded in the concept. Franchisers are fully trained and are locally backed by a national office for technical, operational and management support. Each centre is located in reach of 20,000 people on average.

Ties believes in the project, and no matter how many times he has come to a dead end, he has found a way out. You just have to keep trying harder and harder and, sooner or later, you do succeed.

If there is one thing we can learn from Ties, it is that following your passion is not as difficult as people make it seem. It's as simple as doing what your heart wants to do. Ties has had a very long career, working at a handful of places, learning everywhere, always deciding to pick up something new whenever he wished to, or leaving something and moving on when he felt it was time to do something new. Most people worry too much, wondering what would happen if things go wrong, but Ties took all the risks. And what good is a life if it is one without risks?

He packed his bags and moved to an entirely new country, to try to do something good for the society. A foreign land, a new, low-paying job, unknown language, surrounded by strangers—nothing scared him off. And he succeeded! As a bonus, it brought his family closer together, giving them a chance to start all over again; it was truly an adventure.

His story, among several others in this book, teaches us primarily the attitude of never giving up. Every time Ties completed a course or left a job, he had no clue what to do next. But he always found a way. Attitude is all that matters.

We ask Ties to tell us what has been the one constant force behind him, to make the decisions that he did. What has been his personal philosophy through all of this?

'My drive is to have a positive impact on the lives of as many people as possible. The idea that people can move out of poverty because of the work I do really stimulates me. And my approach is better to try and fail than not try at all.'

## What's New?

Soon after the Unreasonable Institute, the funding for the expansion of NICE was closed for US$4.5 million, consisting of a grant from the European Union (EU) and investment from three large European companies. The expansion project was officially started on 1 October 2011.

Ever since the launch of this project, things started going in the wrong direction. Activities in Tanzania were hampered by their inability to hire a qualified and affordable country manager. Purchase of equipment for new NICE centres was delayed by the tendering procedures required by the EU. And all this time revenues of the existing NICE centres were decreasing as a result of fast changes in the African IT market.

A year into the project a next-generation NICE concept was launched in order to respond to market changes, but NICE had made little progress in scaling up the business. Since the expansion had to be partially funded by the revenues of new NICE centres, the financial basis for the project was no longer there. In July 2013 it was decided to terminate the operations of the international head office in the Netherlands, whilst looking for a solution to continue the subsidiary in the Gambia as an independent company.

Ties closed the office of NICE International in September 2013. The subsidiary in the Gambia was taken over by the management and the subsidiary in Tanzania was liquidated. Ties is now looking for a new role that will allow him to realize his mission of creating massive impact.

# 6

# NEVER QUIT

## ZHAOHUI (ANNA) YANG

Zhaohui (Anna) Yang is CEO and founder of Beijing Green Channel, an innovative China-based company that manufactures and distributes reverse vending machines (RVM) that help increase the recycling of plastic bottles, aluminium cans and other recyclables. It is a high-tech green enterprise under the auspices of the Beijing Academy of Science and Technology. Their vision is to be the research and development leader in the market of RVM for polyethylene terephthalate (PET) bottles and aluminium cans as well as other generated recycling equipment and products, to provide professional recycling solutions for industries and enable a 'win-win' situation between industry and environment.

Anna had ten years of management experience in China prior to her present venture. She served at a diverse set of mid- and senior-level positions: as senior executive of customer relationship management of Beijing DSH (General Motors' sales agency), as general manager of Jiuchuan Intel Education Consultancy and as deputy general manager (in charge of marketing and sales) of Beijing Dongli Construction Group. She also had stints in real estate at Beijing East Lake Villas and education and as an English-language lecturer at the China University of Geosciences.

She has an MBA from the Aston Business School, UK, and an MA and a BA from Beijing University, China.

ANNA WAS born in deep South China, in Putian province where she was raised by her grandparents. And later she went to live with her parents in Beijing, the capital city of China. Both her parents were professors and geologists in the China University of Geosciences. Anna does not have any siblings, since the one-child policy is very prominent in her country, and was especially so around the time she was born.

Anna refuses to answer when asked about the year of her birth. And we allow her this secret. It is not her age, but her entrepreneurial talent and all that she has achieved that we are interested in!

She went to primary school in Beijing and she remembers that time very fondly. 'We had lots of fun. I had a lot of friends. And, you know, I lived on the campus. Since my parents were both professors, we lived on the premises and it was quite nice! Very convenient, of course.

'When I was in secondary school, I dreamt of becoming a diplomat one day. I didn't know exactly what that meant, but I loved painting and music and I wished to travel the world. I wanted to stand on a public stage and represent my country and let the world know what China is really like. That is why I majored in British and American literature.'

After graduating from college, she joined the same institute that her parents were professors in, as a teacher. She taught there for five years. Her parents and grandparents were professors too, so from there, she could see what her future was going to be like. From a lecturer, gaining experience and getting promoted to a professor—she could picture her life.

'I could easily see what was going to happen in the next fifty years. And it was boring. So that was when I realized that the career I was choosing wasn't the one meant for me.'

Throughout her life, she had been surrounded by professors and she did not see herself doing the same. 'I've always tried to do things differently from my parents. Also, while I was teaching at the university, I realized that as far as a career is concerned, all a person can do in this field is wait. Wait to become a professor one day. And I didn't want that.'

'I hate to wait.'

She wanted to do something different—different from her parents, different from what the people around her usually did. Everybody in her family had chosen science as their field of expertise, while Anna had decided to go for arts. But when she still ended up being a lecturer, just like her parents, she decided it was time for her to do something new.

She decided to quit her job. And when she did, she had absolutely no clue what she was going to do next. She just figured she should gain experience. She wanted to try working in local firms, international firms, joint ventures and explore the possibilities. Experience was what she looked for at that point of time.

'My parents didn't think it was a very smart decision. My mother told me that she didn't understand why I needed to quit a good job with a stable salary to struggle doing something else. I didn't know what that *something else* was at that point of time, but what I did know was that I was definitely going to quit the job. My parents thought it was stupid for a girl to quit a job at the university but I was very persistent.'

There was no one on Anna's side when she took the decision of quitting her job. She did not have a friend who supported her (her friends thought she was being absurd quitting her job at the university to start anew—maybe as a secretary in some company) or a mentor of any kind. She was basically on her own.

She started working as an interpreter at a Sino-Danish company dealing with property development known as Beijing East Lake Villas. After a year, she became the personal assistant to the general manager and the deputy general manager of that company. Since the general manager was Chinese and the deputy general manager was Danish, she learnt a lot from the mix of cultures.

From working as a secretary, interpreter and PA in the administration department, Anna later moved on to marketing and sales.

'I don't know if joining that company and working with them was a good decision or bad, but even now, when I'm in low spirits, the only place which can make me happy is that first company I worked with. They cherished my talents, they helped me grow and they offered me a lot of training opportunities.'

The general managers and the vice chairman there motivated Anna to work in marketing and sales and promoted her from the administration department. 'Maybe they were my true mentors, but I didn't realize that at the moment.'

Anna was then headhunted by a local company, Beijing Dongli Construction Group, also dealing with property. She saw it as a good opportunity to diversify and gain some more experience and so she joined that company. She dealt with marketing there and got in touch with some major clients. She had a much more responsible role here. Compared with the first company, where she had been an average employee, here she was the deputy general manager and in charge of marketing.

She worked in that second company for a year and learnt all about project management and how to build up a network, but she didn't enjoy her job as much as she had the first one. Coming from an arts background education-wise, it was a strain leading a team, being logical and responsible all the time.

A client of hers, Tracy (the co-founder of Green Channel, with Anna Yang), told Anna that she was way too qualified to be working for others and motivated her to become an entrepreneur. Anna had never seen herself as someone who would do something of her own, so her whole image of herself changed. Anna began to see herself as Tracy did—creative, innovative and passionate.

What impressed Tracy about Anna was her background—her education.

'My first experience with entrepreneurship was to launch a company dealing with international education consultancy.'

When did this happen?

Her parents thought she was simply crazy. They had no idea how to control her. After quitting her job at the university and then working with a couple of companies dealing with property, Anna had once again quit a promising job and changed her line of work. This time, to do something of her own.

'They thought a girl from an academic background should be more, you know, traditional—a *nice girl*. I'm not saying I'm not nice! But they expected me to be quiet and listen to everything they said. So did my husband.'

Anna had got married while she was teaching at the university. Her husband worked for a state-owned company. Now, he is in charge of five different companies dealing with nuclear power and radiation. Her husband came from a traditional background. It was not easy for the couple to reconcile the career track that Anna had chosen with the ground reality in China, of a business world dominated by men. In the traditional way of thinking, having an independent career (with its own risks and rewards) was often seen as 'at odds' with the woman's role of raising a family, caring for children.

But that never stopped Anna. Tracy and Anna had a lot in common—they had the same values, same principles and they even shared hobbies and tastes.

So this was happening. Tracy convinced Anna to quit her job and later on invested in Anna's company. With the previous experience Anna had in the field of education and the contacts she had in the Beijing market, the company—Jiuchuan Intel Education Consultancy—started off well.

'It was a big deal for me. I never thought I would be the boss!'

They got their company national recognition from the government. The company designed some courses for Chinese students to take before they went overseas to study further. They also helped students with getting the visas and prepared them for a foreign lifestyle and culture they were looking forward to face.

They started making money from the second year. Anna worked with the company for a couple of years. But eventually, all her relentless hard work took a toll on her and she fell sick. The fatigue caused due to lack of sleep (two to three hours every night) and the pressure at work got to her. They had to build a team, starting from one person, going up to twenty and Anna couldn't manage the work–life balance one needs in business. Due to overload, she became too weak to go to work. Once, when she tried to take a lift to the office, she fainted.

Her health deteriorated significantly. Anna and her team started looking for somebody to take over Anna's position. Unfortunately, even though they tried for about eighteen months, they still could not find a good replacement. They decided to shut the company down.

'I learnt a lot from the business—in terms of building up and training teams, HR and project management, setting up networks. I really appreciate Tracy offering me such a kind opportunity in the first place. It essentially helped me realize my personal potential.'

Tracy flew to Oakland, New Zealand, to stay with her family. They had decided to take a break. Anna went to London to study business English proficiency, and stayed there for three months. She remembers it as a happy time.

After her experience there, she wanted to explore more, so she applied for an MBA. She got into Aston Business School (London) and went for it.

'I chose to go there, because I like to mix with other cultures. I also realized that I needed time to review what I had done for the last couple of years. I wanted to do something new. I didn't know *what* at that moment, though!'

But, apparently, she did not know what she had got herself into!

'The first semester was a nightmare for me. I had stayed in London for a few months before and had had a very pleasant experience. Unfortunately, I assumed that staying for a longer time would feel almost the same. Right from the beginning, in the first semester, our course was very extensive. We had lectures, workshops and such—from nine in the morning to nine in the evening. And then, after break, we began our syndicate group discussion, which lasted beyond midnight, till one in the morning. And that was all for nothing—the group was of people from different cultures, some of whom were too democratic, and so there were no conclusions ever. Wow! It was a nightmare for a Chinese.'

'We, Chinese, liked to be result driven. So, we struggled in the syndicate group for the entire semester. I had to handle all the changes, in terms of culture shock, differences of ethics and values . . . and of course differences in the way of communicating. Some British are too democratic and there was no leadership—we were all just rotating, reaching no conclusion in the end.'

It was very challenging for Anna. At one point, she even speculated quitting. When she went back home during her first semester break, she told her family about the problems she was facing. Also, she realized that she did not need the MBA too much either—she had already experienced being the CEO of a start-up. She was not in for the degree, from the beginning; she just wanted to learn. When she found out how difficult the course was proving for her, she figured she could quit it at any moment.

So, she packed her luggage and went back to China for a break, not knowing if she would return to London. Everybody, even Tracy, told Anna that she did not need to struggle like that and suggested that she take a break from it all. Tracy told Anna that even if she learnt Western methodology, she would not be able to apply it completely later, when she was working in her own country—China.

Anna went back to London anyway.

'I just asked a friend to book my ticket back to London. I'm just not somebody who quits.'

She realized that people in London and everybody else in her business school there did not know much about the Chinese culture. Whatever they did know was not very positive either. She thought that being a Chinese, and getting a chance to interact with people outside her China, meant that she was representing her country. And also that it was her responsibility to tell them about the real Chinese culture.

She went to Beijing, Shanghai and a few other places in China during the first semester break and took a lot of pictures to take back to London. She clicked everything she came across—buildings, architecture, local food and local people.

The first thing she did after getting back to London was to organize a seminar, where she explained about the Chinese culture and their way of living in the present. Even if some of the people might not have been interested in knowing or did not believe what she said, she did her part.

'I told myself, "You have to be adaptable and persistent with your decision." I changed my attitude, and it actually worked. Something changed. From the second semester, I became happier, more energetic, started interacting with more people and learnt to ask for help. After that, the rest of the year was a breeze.'

She started touring places around London with her classmates and enjoyed the experience. She learnt about their culture and way of living and started to understand the people there better.

'In China, our way of defining success is having a high position in a company, a lot of money and fame. But in the UK, they measure success by happiness. We can learn something from that. It changed my entire perspective towards life.'

Oh! That's one of the most amazing things someone can learn from an MBA!

'Well, I also learnt cooking!' Anna laughs. 'When I was back in Beijing, I was spoiled by my husband and parents. I was lucky! But when I went to the UK, I had to learn how to cook because we didn't have much time to go out for every meal and the stringent budget—going to a restaurant every day is very expensive. So finally, coming out of the business school, holding my MBA degree, I made fun of myself: I have a certificate—to cook!'

When she was finishing her MBA, she decided to go back to China and put to use everything she had learnt from the course, even though she had no idea what kind of business to start with. She had two targets in her mind—to make a bigger contribution to society and to make sustainable revenue. That was the way she decided to bridge her dream to reality.

But still, she had no idea what to start a business in!

She got back to China in 2005 and spent the first six months visiting her family and friends, all the while looking for something to start a business in. But at that moment, she did not find any satisfying solution. For the time being, she joined General Motors' subsidiary in Beijing. She worked as a customer relationship management executive there. Her line of work changed completely—from education, property management and consultancy to now working for one of the biggest car-manufacturing companies in the world.

'I bought a Buick, because that is one of the products we sold!'

She worked with them for a year, but realized that even though the company is great and working with them was amazing, she could not apply whatever she learnt in Europe if she worked there.

In the time Anna spent in the UK, she found that people there have a strong sense of social awareness, which she found lacking back in China. Her daughter studied in one of the best schools in Beijing and Anna realized that even they did not have any idea about recycling. She noticed that, after parties, they all threw the bottles and cans away, instead of recycling them.

That's how the business idea took seed in her head.

She spent some time with Mr Zhao (who's her partner now), her acquaintance of over ten years, whom she met through her husband and some friends. He was a mechanical engineer, working in the field of radiation application for medical purposes at the time. She discussed her plan with him and they decided to start a company together.

They did some research over the Internet, looking for machines used for recycling. During this time, Anna began to feel the first bouts of excitement—she would finally be able to apply in her business everything she had learnt.

In 2007, they launched Green Channel.

They put their own money—US$30,000—in the business. Anna had saved some money over time, and her partner put in his part and they got the company going.

'With the vision of reshaping the system, we designed an innovative recycling medium. We developed a recycling platform—which involved more people, had greater output—and, at the same time, we passed on informative messages about recycling, thus spreading our vision.' They also gave away rewards and small gifts, all the while concentrating on keeping the business module sustainable.

They started with two people—Anna and Zhao—and now employ twelve. In the first year of the company, they designed and tested different types of prototypes, participated in several international exhibitions held in Beijing and tried to learn more and more, so that they could develop the best possible business model. From the second year, they started trying to sell the machines. It was still in the pilot stage and not the standard commercial product, because of a lack of funds and human resources.

They designed an ideal distribution channel—retail stores, schools, gasoline industry—and it took a year to come together. It was a challenging period for them. The cans and bottles go into the machine and are sorted out into separate containers. They come out recycled and compressed and then they get the money refunded. Anna says the smaller ones are worth five cents and the bigger worth a dime. Taken together—they add up to becoming a large amount.

All this while, they kept travelling to educate people about recycling and to try to change the recycling supply chain. Not many people cared in the beginning. Anna and Zhao discovered that, in the existing system, the only resources they would ever get were from the government and organizations in the distribution channel.

'All we got in the first year was no, no and no. Everywhere from everyone. We kept working anyway. For me, anyway, the journey to the destination is the most exciting part of the process!'

They believed they could work it all out, in time. They did not give up and kept working. They were working for a cause and had belief in it. How could they give up?

They got their first order, by the end of the first year.

'First year—ten units. Second year—fifty-three. So that's progress.'

Who are their prime customers?

First and foremost—the government. They are putting an emphasis on recycling and are keen on it, hence becoming one of the most important customers of Green Channel. Second—and one Anna says they need to cover more—the beverage industry. They are very relevant to the recycling scene and have a huge involvement in the same. Third—the petroleum industry; in the future, Anna has plans to install recycling machines at petrol stations.

That's the first revenue stream of Green Channel: selling the machines. The second is through tailor-made advertisements, for which they collaborate with ad agencies. They provide the machines in designed distribution channels for use and later share the revenue generated with the ad agencies.

'The revenue generated from the advertisements should cover the manufacture amount of the machine and also the maintenance services we provide.'

In 2011, Anna applied to the Unreasonable Institute and it was then that Green Channel got associated with them.

By the year 2020, where does Anna see this business going?

'It's a long way to go,' Anna says, poring over the question. 'We'll definitely increase our recycling rates. In terms of scaling up, we want to spread nationally—throughout China—as a marketing leader in providing recycling machines. We would like Green Channel to occupy, say, 60 to 70 per cent of the market share.'

The biggest challenge Green Channel has faced and still faces is raising money to scale up. Also, their machines need to be more reliable, durable and cost-effective at the same time. They also need to speed up; even though the company is doing fine for now, a higher output is desirable.

'When people realize they can make money from this module, maybe the next day we wake up, we find a number of copycats at the door. It happens everywhere; it's a risky business. And given the population China has, it won't be a surprise if more than a few people start stealing our business model.'

Fortunately, Green Channel has four patents and has also won national recognition. In the future, they also want to expand outside China.

'We need to change the view of people outside our country of the term "Chinese product". People say Chinese products are low quality, cheap and bulk manufactured without quality control. I don't think I want people to think about our products that way. I want to change that view.'

Green Channel wants to prove that their products are innovative and of good quality. They want to come up with an attractive design and brand their product too.

We have seen Anna go from being a teacher to an employee with a regular job, to an entrepreneur, then back to being a student and a successful entrepreneur again. All through this, what has been her personal philosophy, her way of looking at things and handling them?

'I've always tried to make the best of what I had. Being a girl, I had a chance to get a good education and I decided to do as good as I can to use it in the most productive way. Rather than being narrow-minded, I look for expanding my horizons.'

> 'Green is harmonious, peaceful and integrates culture. I want to create a greener world.'

Green Channel wants to create a healthy and beautiful world for the next generation, and the ones after that. With a clear vision, it marches ahead with confidence, to make the world that we live in a better place.

## What's New?

Since starting off, Anna has faced several problems and obstacles, one after the other. But she never once gave up. That's the sign of a good leader. She tried her hand at everything that caught her interest, never missing out on any chance. She took risks, again and again, quitting good and respectable jobs to struggle and find out what she really wanted to do in life. It's not like she was always lucky; she surely wasn't. With every risk, she was faced with a number of new problems.

But struggling is a part of every entrepreneur's story. And what's a good story without each of the key elements?

Anna's journey inspires us, makes us believe in the power within every person. Green Channel started off with a lot of lows, followed by highs and finally took wings.

All throughout, and even now, Anna is very clear about her vision: 'I started Green Channel to increase the younger generation's awareness about protecting the earth. I want to help cultivate an internal green culture of caring for the earth and influence more and more people . . . I'm chasing the dream of improving China to a greener, greater and more sustainable, innovative country that can rock the world!'

# 7

# WORK HARD, DON'T STOP

## RAJ JANAGAM

Raj Janagam is the twenty-four-year-old co-founder and CEO of Cycle Chalao!, which was one of India's first and fastest growing bike-sharing programmes. The Cycle Chalao! model is simple: they rent out bicycles at major railway stations and public places for a small fee. Members can pick up the bicycles at one station and drop them off at any other station. With pilot research and operations in Mumbai and Pune, they are looking to scale up to every city in India, in partnership with local city governments. Raj has been featured by *Forbes*, *Fast Company* and *Outlook* business magazines. He lives by the mantra, 'Take ownership of your life. If you don't, someone else will!'

AT FIRST glance, it is difficult to imagine that the twenty-four-year-old you are shaking hands with is anybody out of the ordinary. Raj looks and talks like a typical young Mumbaikar—mobile phone in hand, quickly cycling through different topics, never resting. As the conversation unfolds, though, you soon realize you are in the presence of an extraordinary young man. Raj is making his own path, shaping his own destiny, as he creates one of the world's largest bike-sharing systems, right here in India.

Raj's story begins like many other Mumbai kids'. His grandfather came to Mumbai from Andhra Pradesh and his father followed him there to improve their fortunes. His father, originally from a small farming community called Himmatpeth in Andhra Pradesh, came to the city of dreams to look for work—and found it as a schoolteacher at a government school in Worli. His mother, who never went to school beyond class three, is a housewife. Raj lived with his parents and two sisters in a place called Gopal Nagar in Mumbai. Mumbaikars would recognize this place as adjacent to the huge Doordarshan TV tower and also for having the dubious distinction of being Mumbai's second-largest slum, after Dharavi.

Like thousands of other slum children, Raj has childhood experiences of living together with family and relatives in cramped spaces, of community toilets flooded during the monsoon. Money was always a problem, compounded by his family's insistence on taking on the financial responsibilities of their distant relatives. 'We borrowed money to support my mother's brothers . . . and some of them blew the money on drink . . . It was not the easiest of times,' recollects Raj.

One of Raj's earliest memories is of fighting over the ownership of a pencil with another boy in school, in class two. Unknown to Raj, the boy's mother was the school principal. For Raj, it did not end well—he ran home and never returned to the same school. An early lesson in whom to pick fights with!

Thereafter, till class five, he was homeschooled by his father, only going to school for exams. When he did make a return (to a different school this time!) in class five, Raj enjoyed his time, making many friends and doing well in studies. He took great pride in being the 'top ranker' in class, and his father tried his best to encourage his reading—buying him quiz books and comics.

'I remember eagerly awaiting and devouring *Tinkle* comics. My favourite was Suppandi . . .'

In school, he was highly respected—a teacher's son and a 'scholar'. Most of the kids were from the slums; many were children of mill workers of the area and shared similar problems in life to Raj. He found he could relate and develop good friendships. Especially after class eight, he started participating in many extracurricular activities—drama in particular caught his fancy. Throughout school, apart from getting the 'first rank' Raj had no ambition, no notion of what to do next in life. In his free time, Raj did what many kids of the '90s would relate to—he watched Doordarshan in the afternoon, and had particular cartoon shows he would watch for one hour after school.

His father aspired for him to become an IAS officer, with all the prestige and respect in the community that this would bring.

At this time, Raj had two formative experiences. Encouraged by his mother, he had enrolled for a Bhagavadgita recitation competition. 'This was serious stuff. I learnt, by heart, the eleventh chapter, end to end!' remembers Raj. It was hard work, early morning practice, learning all the lines, all the shlokas, by rote. His efforts were rewarded by a win in the contest, and he imbibed a virtue he has never lost since then: 'Work hard, don't ever stop.' This would, in time, stand him in good stead with his own venture.

A second, more unpleasant, experience also occurred at the same time. Raj was studying in a Telugu-medium school. In classes eight, nine and ten, the classes in school were segregated into two—'lower level' for all the vernacular medium students like him and 'higher level' for everyone in the English medium. The higher level English students and even the teachers seemed to always look down upon the lower level Telugu students. Merely by virtue of the language he spoke—or rather, did not speak!—he was 'lower' in some way. This struck him as unjust and inherently unfair. At the time, though, there was nothing he could do but carry this feeling of injustice with him.

In the tenth board exams, Raj scored 83 per cent. This was a good result but Raj was still scared—some of his friends were in the above 85 per cent boat. He was not sure where he would be able to secure admissions next. He eventually selected and secured a science seat in Andhra Education Society. Junior college—classes eleven and twelve—is when Raj started coming into his own. He had his first love affair—and that, too, with a girl from the 'higher level'! It was a good time—he spent a lot of time with his girlfriend and was pleasantly surprised when she started working on her Telugu to improve it.

He was not doing too well in his courses in college though. Very quickly, Raj realized that science—physics, chemistry and the like—was not his cup of tea. He had enrolled for coaching for engineering entrance exams, but dropped out. Instead, he became fascinated by the political issues of the time. He devoured newspapers, formed strong opinions about city-development plans, the conditions of the slums, of the actions (or lack of action!) of local politicians. In particular, he was struck by how many newspapers' coverage of the slums painted these as negative places, to be razed and removed from Mumbai. For Raj, this brought to the fore turbulent feelings—he belonged to the slums and here he was, seemingly personally unwanted by the city. This phase in his life had more questions and not many answers. What was sure for Raj, though, was that science did not hold the answers. He moved over to social sciences, opting for a Bachelor of Arts at Ruia College. He desperately wanted to study political science but, eventually, the political science quota was full and Raj had to select an alternative. So he majored in philosophy. And had a fantastic time.

In the rarefied atmosphere of his new surroundings, Raj blossomed. For the next three years at Ruia College in

Mumbai, Raj's world grew by leaps and bounds. He was now mingling with students from diverse backgrounds—kids who came to college in their own chauffeur-driven cars to others like him, from humbler backgrounds—but everyone seemed to be doing something. There were many interesting things happening in college—extempore debates, drama and elocution contests. For Raj, this was a tremendous experience. Crucially, in his coursework, he opted for one course at the Centre for Slum Studies, taught by Medha Somaiya, the wife of a prominent politician in Mumbai, Kirit Somaiya. For the first time, Raj formally learnt about the development sector, of social entrepreneurship, about how to quantify impact. Importantly, he could now frame the issues in their proper context, explain and argue points logically with experts in the field. With his own experiences of growing up in relative poverty, this was a strong foundation to set out on the path of a social entrepreneur. But he still did not have a clue what he was going to do in life.

Meanwhile, another strong influence came from a different source: the National Cadet Corps (NCC), of which Raj was an enthusiastic and willing member. The NCC is a volunteer military organization that provides university students basic arms and military training. Importantly, it provides discipline, structure and invaluable leadership training. He had been enrolled there by his sister and it was here that Raj grew confident in public speaking, organizing events, leading teams of cadets. He grew to love the NCC enough to give serious consideration to the thought of applying to get into the Indian Army. Particularly strong influences with the NCC for Raj were his instructors Mr Varpe, Mr Borase and Mr Hadavle. They had strong army-officer traits, with confident leadership qualities, and a strong, clear value system that manifested in even the way they walked and talked and went about their daily life. Raj wanted to be a man in their mould. In time, he became a leader of a contingent at Ruia College and rose through the ranks to manage fifty-two cadets, generally deploying them for various volunteer social-service activities in the area. Raj also got to travel extensively around the country, attending parades, events and conferences. It brought about a lot of exposure to the scale and diversity of India to the young man from the slums of Mumbai. A striking memory of his, however, remains of how he returned from an NCC camp in Punjab to the news in Mumbai that his girlfriend had broken up with him! His busy schedule had come at a cost.

While depressed about this, Raj continued to be heavily engaged with different activities outside of college in his time at Ruia. In his second year, he recollects, he only attended one class in total! Even in that class, he came late. The professor, irritable, said, 'Get out if you don't want to be in class. I'll give you full attendance credit.' Raj got out and got the full attendance credit.

Even though the term 'social entrepreneur' was still alien to him, it was now clear to him that he wanted to do something in that world, be of some public service. In his third and final year at Ruia, he decided to give his courses a chance and attended more classes and became well versed with philosophy, his major. It helped that the professor—Vice Principal Vatsala Pai—was very good. Raj was now in the world of evaluating the theories behind right and wrong, choices people and civilizations make, decision-making and morality. Heavy stuff! Raj loved it. He especially grew to enjoy discourses on Western philosophy. Socrates, in particular, grew on him, and he found he could relate to this ancient Greek philosopher more than many of the teachings of Indian mysticism.

While at Ruia, Raj had become the general secretary of the college film society, whose mandate was to promote viewership of art movies. Raj, always the one to think big and jump in with both feet, decided to organize a national-level film festival. He worked with distributors in Delhi and arranged for the rights to screen the films from the World Social Forum, Rio de Janeiro. It was difficult, and hard work but his team pulled it off eventually. Various award-winning foreign-language films were screened, and the festival attracted serious film watchers.

Around this time, Medha Somaiya, suggested he take up a research project at Partners for Urban Knowledge, Action and Research (PUKAR). They could provide a small grant of ₹60,000 (US$1200) to take up a research project that affected the city. Raj took up the project and chose as his research topic 'Injustice of Studying in a Vernacular Medium'. This was an issue close to his heart. The research took him to different parts of Mumbai, especially to Dharavi, where he interviewed students, parents, teachers and government leaders. While, on the one hand, parents were reluctant to sever their children's ties with their mother tongues, they could clearly see the opportunities their children were deprived of once they were starved of English-language education. Raj believes that a middle ground would be to have all science and mathematics education in English, from a young age. There is, as with many complex issues, not a simple answer.

As Raj immersed himself in these issues, he learnt the methodology and process behind the research and was eventually approached by Pooja Warier of UnLtd India, a social-business incubator in Mumbai, to consider applying for a fellowship at UnLtd India. Meanwhile, Raj came to know about Dr Meena Galliara, chairperson for an MBA programme in social entrepreneurship. Raj could not afford the fees but thanks to the guidance of Dr Meena Galliara, HOD Social Enterprise Cell, Narsee Monjee Institute of Management Studies (NMIMS) University, he secured a scholarship that gave him entry into a part-time social entrepreneurship. And so began the next chapter in his life. Both Pooja Warier and Meena Galliara would become mentors and offer key support in his journey later with Cycle Chalao!

Through his college years, the situation at home had deteriorated—the family finances were worse than ever, and there was no money forthcoming from his parents. His parents and relatives could not understand why he needed to study further and were keen for Raj to 'knuckle down' to a steady job. Raj had to take his education in his own hands. To support himself, he used the stipends from the NCC, money from competitions he won and borrowed money from his sisters. He also began working part-time as a reporter for newspapers. Each article printed would fetch ₹250 to ₹500 (five to ten US dollars). Here, Raj found opportunity to cover the social issues close to his heart. Also, he grew increasingly familiar with the Right to Information Act (RTI) and filed numerous applications for information on suspect civic projects. He also was hired by an upcoming Telugu political party called Loksatta as a promoter to lead a youth campaign. The salary was ₹8000 (US$180) per month. At this organization, Raj developed a national-level campaign called '*Bharat Jodo Andolan*'. This was inspired by Baba Amte's work. At the time, Raj Thackeray, the leader of a right-wing political party called the Shiv Sena in Mumbai, was strongly advocating that non-Maharashtrians leave Mumbai. Raj's plan involved rail trips where young people from different districts would come together and visit different states. This was the first-ever major campaign of this nature for Loksatta. It was turning into a great success. And here was a seventeen-year-old greenhorn leading it! Raj was working eighteen-hour days, and was therefore aghast when his bosses at Loksatta decided to install someone more senior to run the show. Frustrated, Raj and eight of his colleagues quit the organization.

Eventually, this became an on-going campaign—'One India One People'—for Loksatta. But at the time, Raj felt robbed of all the hard work he and his young colleagues had put in. Another lesson in life!

While all this was happening, he continued his part-time education at NMIMS. Here, the class came from very different worlds—from fifty-year-old corporate executives to heads of charitable foundations, to raw youths with very little real-world experience, looking for jobs and direction. It was a very good environment for peer-to-peer learning.

With Raj's dynamism and exploits, there was no shortage of work for him. While studying at NMIMS, while he was speaking at a Child Relief and You (CRY)—organized panel, he was approached by Sanyogita Dhamdhere, from the Centre for Advocacy and Research (CFAR). 'You should work for us,' she said. And so he did.

The job was simple. He had to scour through all the Mumbai newspapers and report a summary of all the news about health issues like HIV and AIDS on a daily basis to their Pune office. CFAR wanted someone intelligent to do this, and Raj was only too willing to have someone pay him ₹8000 a month to read newspapers! He loved his job—devouring eighteen newspapers a day, and would probably have done it for free if asked. He worked at this for eight months until his next adventure began: Cycle Chalao!

Raj had no particular affinity towards bicycles. Although he owned a bicycle, he was by no means an avid cyclist. The idea for Cycle Chalao! came to him not from any passion for cycling but from a real-life need.

Raj used to commute from his house to his college by train and autorickshaw. The train journey from Elphinstone Road Station to Ville Parle Station was the easy part (by Mumbai standards, of course). The frustration for Raj was the problems with the autorickshaws to get from or to the local railway stations. Firstly, there would be long queues for the rickshaws. Secondly, the rickshaws used to get stuck in unending traffic jams near the stations. Raj was often late for class, being stuck in an autorickshaw. And it drove him nuts.

Once, when on the receiving end of not-so-kind words from a particularly irate Raj, a rickshaw driver made a spur-of-the-moment comment: *'Agar itna hi ghai mein ho, to khud ka cycle kyun nahi chelate shahar mein!'* (If you are in such a hurry, you should ride your own bicycle in this city!)

The comment stuck with Raj through the day at college. He played with the idea in his head. He could not focus on his classes for that day, as various possibilities came to him. The best cities in the world had bicycle-sharing programmes— bicycles which could be rented and used by commuters on an ad-hoc basis. Paris, Copenhagen, Montreal, Amsterdam—why not Mumbai?

He wondered why no one had started a bicycle-sharing scheme in Mumbai. This was the question he went and asked Dr Meena Galliara, his mentor at NMIMS.

'Why don't you find out why? And while you are at it, write a concept note on your plan!' was her response. And so he did.

His concept note, circulated amongst the faculty and students of NMIMS, was very well received. 'Do it!' was the unanimous response from his professors and peers. And so he did.

The basic model from that concept note remains unchanged. The core premise was that people should be able to pick up a bicycle from any point and return it at any point, and pay a small fee as rental—either daily or weekly or monthly. This was the essence of bicycle sharing. But the challenge was making it work on the ground.

Raj envisaged establishing parking stations at railway stations and major public places. While everyone was well aware of the polluting nature of vehicles in major Indian cities, this never entered the picture for Raj as a serious motivation for the venture. He was well aware of the ground realities that it had to serve the primary motive of addressing the transportation needs of users, first and foremost. Without this, it would not work, regardless of its other benefits.

From the very beginning, his thinking was tilted more towards creating value for the customer, rather than the 'non-profit foundation' mindset. Perhaps this had a lot to do with the lesson learnt in his personal life and previous job experiences: it was better to be financially independent and capable of standing on your own two feet, whether as a person or as an organization!

There was a lot of research—a lot of groundwork—to be done before he could proceed. He had no idea how to go about starting a business, and certainly no idea of what it took to launch a bicycle-sharing scheme. To start with, he took the idea to the PUKAR group. This was a group that had previously helped him with a fellowship that made his ends meet through college. The director of PUKAR, Anita Deshmukh, put Raj in touch with the right people to get the critical market data and information he needed to get started. Especially helpful was Rahul Srivastava, a correspondent at *Mumbai Mirror*, a news daily.

Putting together a team of volunteers, Raj interviewed 350 people on the streets of Mumbai to check the viability of the bicycle-sharing model. He got an enthusiastic response but also some reservations about the safety of using bicycles in a city such as Mumbai. He took his findings to Pooja Warier at UnLtd India. The folks at UnLtd India were very supportive and agreed to grant Raj ₹60,000 to test the model on the ground. Raj was ecstatic. Sixty thousand rupees may not sound like a lot of money but it was enough to get things started. Especially if, as Raj thought, you could keep your costs to a minimum!

Raj recruited a team of twenty-one volunteers (friends and students) and got to work. From consumer surveys, they decided to price the bicycle-sharing service at ₹150 per month (about three US dollars). While many MBA students were learning theory, Raj was busy building real-life business plans, and loving it. The team's plan was to have a bicycle facility at every local railway station in Mumbai, with fifty bicycles for each facility. Each facility would have one attendant as well as a relationship with a local bicycle-repair shop to maintain the bicycles. There would also be four similar stations around each railway station, to service major office and commercial areas. The numbers added up well on Raj's Excel sheet: Mumbai had 150 railway stations, there would be five bicycle stations in and around each railway station, and each bicycle station would have fifty bicycles, with each bicycle earning the venture ₹150 per month. This meant that there was an addressable market of ₹56.25 lakh a month (about US$112,000) for the business in Mumbai alone! And after that, there would be Bangalore, Delhi, Kolkata, Chennai and so on. The costs would be the initial capital costs of the bicycles and the recurring monthly costs of paying employees and maintaining the bicycles. The financial model was coming together well.

Apart from the basic 'per-month' model, they also decided to offer 'per-day' and 'per-week' plans, and introduced a simple coupon-based system to make the payment system work.

Of all the volunteers, Raj and two others—Jui Gangan and Jyotika Bhatia—decided to take the venture up full-time and get incubated at UnLtd India. The target was to launch a pilot project of the venture—named in the monsoon of 2009. After much deliberation, the trio decided to name the venture 'Cycle Chalao!'

They soon hit their first hurdle: they ran out of money. The ₹60,000 from UnLtd India had been exhausted in the initial research and setting up the registration for the venture as a charitable trust. While they had identified, based on their research, a good area to launch the pilot—Mulund, a suburb of Mumbai, and a friendlier place than many in Mumbai for cycling—they had no money to buy bicycles!

Their plan was to raise money for sixty bicycles—a budget of about ₹4 lakh (about US$8000). While scouting for donations, it soon became apparent to the young entrepreneurs that it was not realistic if they wanted to try to raise this money as a donation. They revised their expectations to ₹2 lakh (thirty bicycles) and eventually managed to achieve their target thanks to a loan (with a small interest rate of 8 per cent) provided by Vijay Sathey, a local business person and prominent member of the Parleshwar Rotary Club, who saw potential in the idea to improve the local traffic situation.

For technical know-how on choice of and regular maintenance of the bicycles, the team approached Bhaskar Asgaonkar. Bhaskar was a local celebrity of sorts, having been covered in the local press for the invention of a mobile charger that worked with a bicycle. In the initial stages, Bhaskar was a great source of help to Raj and his team, helping them with the operations of the pilot.

Mulund was proving to be the right choice for the pilot.

The location was near Kelkar College, and the team decided to focus on students as the customers. This was especially useful because students instantly saw value in the offering and were early adopters. Also, ID verification was simple with the student's college ID cards and the chances of theft reduced considerably. In fact, not a single bicycle was stolen. Just to be safe, Raj had them insured from Oriental Insurance.

The bicycles themselves—thirty of them—had been purchased from S.K. brand of cycles, a local brand that was a spin-off from Hero Cycles. The main allure for this choice was the lower cost—₹2700 each (about fifty-four US dollars). In addition, Bhaskar had also arranged a tricycle that could ferry five bicycles at a time. This was needed to 'recycle' the bicycles from one station to the other, to balance out the supply. There was also a two-seater tandem bicycle, used for promoting the pilot in Mulund.

Everyone was doing everything at this stage, with the real buzz of a new venture. There was no clarity in the roles and therein one problem emerged. Bhaskar, who was initially very helpful, began to lose enthusiasm for the venture and, soon, conflicts broke out within. Bhaskar left the team.

In addition, the S.K. brand of bicycles was living up to its low cost—its quality was suspect and they required more maintenance than the team had foreseen. There were constant breakages. It was all a learning experience.

Raj had managed to hire seven students as interns from YMT College of Management. This was a great resource to have, and, best of all, it was free! The team scurried around frenetically, getting permissions for space, buying bicycles, having fun.

The launch of Cycle Chalao! in Mulund was a huge success. The buzz they had created with the local press and their tandem bicycle promotions led to a sell-out of their entire inventory by day two of the pilot. All their bicycles were booked for the coming month, and they ended up having more than 250 registered rides on their books by the time the month was up. The team was elated!

But despite the fantastic response from customers, a lot of work remained. The first issue was the safety of the bicycles. They were being kept in the open and Raj was uneasy about this arrangement. Being well networked with the local leaders in Mulund, Raj tried to find a solution to this problem by way of parking space at one of the Brihanmumbai Municipal Corporation (BMC, the municipal body of Mumbai) lots. Eventually, with Manish Motwani, the Chair of Global Warming at the Rotary Club, arranging meets with politicians and the BMC ward office, a solution was finally found. A local business person and person of note, Sunit Bhagat, offered his own space—a parking lot for the night to lock away the bicycles safely. In addition, Raj employed security for the night.

Next, Raj was eager to find additional sources of revenue for the business. While the sell-out of his inventory of thirty bicycles on day two was promising, this was only generating about ₹4500 a month, minus the operating costs, security, maintenance, downtime of the bicycles due to repair and interest on the loan taken to finance the capital costs. The team was not drawing any salaries and, unless alternative sources of revenue could be found, it did not look likely that they would at any time! Raj's plan was to get businesses to advertise on the bicycles. To use the bicycles as moving billboards. To this end, he had the thirty bicycles outfitted with custom fibre rear mudguards, specifically fitted to carry a hoarding. Here was a space for advertisements. Surely, this had to be a better solution for advertisers than dead static hoardings by the roadside?

Then came an unexpected problem: permits. It turned out that a special permission was needed from the BMC to offer commercial hoarding space in the city. Of course, there was no specific clarity on getting this for hoardings on bicycles and therein lay the problem: they needed to get the permits but there was no one in the BMC who was willing to issue one for bicycles! This was typical inertia of a large bureaucracy, and was very frustrating for the young Cycle Chalao! team. They had found advertisers ready to back them, but were now faced with the prospect of long delays as their application waited the right set of approvals in the BMC office. A 'babu' in an office would decide the fate of their business. Every day the file lay in the office, Cycle Chalao! was losing potential revenue.

They were helped by the fact that they had an extremely lean cost structure. Their operations were as bare-bones as one could get. They owned no physical structure. Their only assets, apart from the bicycles, were one chair and one promotional umbrella, for shade. Everything else was either free (like the parking space, volunteers and interns as staff) or for relatively low 'Indian prices' (e.g., the night-time security, cycle-repair services, et cetera). And it helped that the founders were not drawing any salaries!

There were 'clean-up marshals' on the streets of Mumbai, whose job was to take down illegal advertising hoardings.

They would not have allowed Cycle Chalao! bicycles to carry commercial messages of any kind without the requisite BMC approvals, and there was still no response from the BMC to their application. Raj was getting nervous and took his problem to Manish Motwani, from the Rotary Club. Motwani was sympathetic and decided to intervene. 'Don't worry, just go ahead and do it in Mulund at least. We need you!' he said to Raj. He would try to get the team the permissions in Mulund at least.

Eventually, a solution was found around the impasse with the BMC. Cycle Chalao! was in business! Their first advertiser client was the Working Women's Association, who wanted to promote a campaign of theirs along with the Asian Heart Hospital. The team was overjoyed! They could pay themselves their first salaries totalling ₹30,000 from the proceeds. It felt good.

Gradually, they arrived at a standard pricing model for advertisers. They charged ₹600 per cycle per month.

A good thing that had happened was the very favourable press coverage that Cycle Chalao! got, right from the beginning. This was always a good thing, as far as advertisers were concerned.

Raj talked to many potential clients, and faced many polite noes (and some not so polite ones too!) for every successful meeting. It was tough going. Advertising on bicycles was a new concept in India, and what really complicated the matter was Cycle Chalao!'s 'start-up' nature. Being a small, nascent venture with only thirty bicycles, large advertisers were reluctant to put their rupees in them. They would need scale, but they could never get to scale without the advertising money! Raj and the team struggled with the problem.

An unexpected ray of hope came from a different source. They began to get a lot of interest from special events. The first-ever Cyclothon was held in Mumbai (where a popular film star—Salman Khan—made appearances on a bicycle, to large, cheering crowds), and the event organizers were short of bicycles. Could they rent Cycle Chalao! bicycles? They were ready to offer premium rates.

Similarly, other events came along—'Car Free Day', rallies, races and so forth—and Cycle Chalao! started to get a steady set of clients who paid premium rates. It was good business, but there was a problem. Since they had only a limited set of thirty bicycles, every bicycle rented to the events meant one or more irate regular customers, who were faced with a diminished supply for regular rides. To solve the problem, Raj decided that the 'events' would only get Cycle Chalao! bicycles on weekends. On weekdays, when students and office workers had to go around, there had to be continuity to the supply and this regular operation could not be disrupted by ad hoc events. It was a good decision and a good compromise.

By this time, Raj was thinking of scaling. The first step he took was to reduce dependence on volunteers, and try to formalize Cycle Chalao! operations. In particular, contracting the 'spot-boy' job of collecting cash and that of maintaining the bicycles to a security agency proved to be a success. The security guards proved to be stable hires, and things went smoother than with volunteers or local part-time youth hires.

At this stage, they were still a lean operation. Thirty bicycles meant about ₹20,000 in monthly revenue. Costs were low—only ₹1000 per month for maintenance for all thirty bicycles, small salaries to the security guard and 'spot boy'. Raj was satisfied that he had arrived at a model that could scale. Cycle Chalao! hired its first full-time execution team: Prashant, Sagar and Jaideep joined, freeing up Raj and Jui's time to look at the strategic issues around scaling. Roles became more defined. The execution team managed operations on a day-to-day basis. Jui looked at social media and partnerships, generating partnerships and building the brand. Raj focused on raising funding, developing the strategy for scaling and getting in more advertising clients.

Cycle Chalao!'s sustainability was based on the advertising model. Without large advertising contracts, there was no possibility to scale. Raj realized this and tried very hard to get two or three strategic partners on board. He knocked on the doors of many agencies. However, he kept hitting the same chicken-and-egg problem that many entrepreneurs face: people would only back him if he was big and he could only become big if people backed him. To move to the next level of scale, Raj made an operational plan to expand to 100 bicycles, and decided to start looking for angel/venture capital funding of up to ₹30 lakh. To make equity investments feasible for private investors, he registered a private limited company—Impact Carbocuts Pvt. Ltd. This holding company would own and manage the Cycle Chalao! brand and operations.

He had the core of the plan already in place: processes, know-how and a working proof of concept in Mulund. He needed, however, to buy more bicycles and invest in docking stations and technology to manage operations efficiently, to replicate the processes from his Mulund stations to other parts of Mumbai. However, like the advertisers, investors too were demanding scale before they would invest. With the current level of Cycle Chalao!, angel investors were demanding about 25 per cent to even 75 per cent of the company. This did not seem reasonable to Raj, as with this kind of a deal, they would be too handicapped to scale in the future. However, he could also see the chicken-and-egg problem that the investors saw—they were willing to invest in something of value but to become something of value needed investment. Cycle Chalao! would need to become much bigger before it became a viable value proposition for large investors *and* large advertisers.

A way around the chicken-and-egg problem of performance and scale was a different kind of approach—become partners with the government! Because of the green nature of the venture, the local media coverage of Cycle Chalao! had generated a lot of interest from civic societies and local politicians. Perhaps there was a financial partnership possible with government agencies?

After all, in the long term, Raj had no doubt that bicycle sharing is a city government responsibility. In most cities where these schemes have been successful around the world, the ventures are run and backed by local city governments. Because cycling needs a particular infrastructure—cycle paths, urban planning, financial incentives to switch to bicycles over other polluting means of transport, et cetera—it needs the backing of the city and, as such, can only truly be a large-scale, impactful venture if there are the right partnerships in place with the government.

However, 'partnerships with the government' was easier said than done. Although Raj met with many government officials, there was never any tangible outcome of the meetings, and after three months of trying he had nothing particularly positive to report from his dealings with the government. He had not expected too much—after all, it would take time for city or state or Central governments to move on anything of this nature—and all he could do was keep talking, keep advocating and, in the meantime, keep surviving in Mulund with Cycle Chalao!

In May 2011, Cycle Chalao!'s performance in Mumbai attracted the team at the Unreasonable Institute. After successfully qualifying through the Unreasonable Marketplace, Raj was ready to fly to Boulder, Colorado, to attend the institute with twenty-five other entrepreneurs from around the world! It was an exciting time for him personally. However, no sooner was he in the US than news came through that his efforts to generate interest in bicycle-sharing schemes in the government were paying off, and that there was likely to be an important meeting on this called by the urban development ministry in Delhi.

By this time, Raj had spent a few days in Boulder, with his newfound friends. The date for the meeting in Delhi came through. It was imperative that Raj be present there. This could be 'make or break' for the future of Cycle Chalao!

A problem was that Raj did not have the money to get back to India at such short notice. The round-trip ticket from Boulder to Delhi cost US$2000. Raj—the bootstrapped entrepreneur!—did not have this cash in his bank account, and did not want to jeopardize the operations of Cycle Chalao! to get the money. This was when something truly extraordinary took place.

One of the people Raj had made friends with in the first week at the Unreasonable Institute was Ties Kroezen, managing director of NICE. Ties was a forty-something professional consultant turned entrepreneur from the Netherlands, who was setting up a series of ICT centres in Africa. You've read his story earlier in this book!

Ties saw the urgency of Raj's situation and leapt to the rescue. Using his own credit card, he quickly bought Raj's ticket for US$2000 to India, patted him on the back and said, 'Go, Raj!'

Then a call was made to the Unreasonable community—the people of Boulder, who were supporting the activities of the institute—to contribute generously to fund Raj's trip. Within a few days, individual contributions from patrons and supporters of the Unreasonable Institute totalled US$2000.

And Ties could breathe a sigh a relief. 'Now I can afford to tell the story to my wife!' he joked. What was amazing was not only the impromptu support at some personal financial risk by one entrepreneur for another, but then, later, the generosity of the crowd, to raise US$2000 in less than a week.

Raj recollects and smiles. 'This is the kind of thing that makes you happy to be alive, makes you proud to be human. I am proud to call Ties my friend, and cannot thank the people of Boulder enough for their kindness.' Raj took the air ticket, flew to Delhi and made a passionate case for bicycle sharing to the government in Delhi. In part due to Raj's efforts, along with the other advocates and civic leaders' voices, the ministry of urban development announced a proposal whereby 50 per cent of all costs for bicycle-sharing schemes would be funded by the government. As with government proposals, there were complexities involved, with different responsibilities borne by different agencies within the government structure. But in principle, this paved the way for a massive scaling of the bicycle-sharing concept in India. It was epic.

Raj is aware that a possibility exists that the government could take over his beloved Cycle Chalao! His view is surprisingly pragmatic: 'At the end of the day, what matters is that the concept reaches the masses. That is what impact means. For cycle sharing, all the successes—Rome, Copenhagen, Amsterdam, Montreal—have come with support from the government. We are solving a complex urban problem, and you need the government to be heavily involved to tackle a problem of this nature. I would not be sad even if I did not personally own a stake in Cycle Chalao!, so long as bicycle sharing became adopted across all Indian cities. If we don't move to cycling now, it might be too late. Indian cities cannot take any further increase in the number of cars and autorickshaws!'

Raj is a believer in being part of the system. At the fledgling age of twenty-four he already has an active presence in local politics (he is an elected youth representative) in his ward in Mumbai and retains his zeal for public service that began with his college days. Being part of the system means reconciling the two apparently disparate worlds of being of social service and being a successful business person. Raj is a social entrepreneur and seems at consummate ease playing these two roles at once. 'With NGOs, I saw a huge gap. I think there has to be an alternative, a better way of doing social good. Perhaps social entrepreneurship is the way?' he ventures.

For now, with Cycle Chalao!'s destiny in his hands, he wants to scale. With policy support fast moving on to his side, he wants to be a leader in bicycle sharing in all cities in the Indian subcontinent. The road ahead for Cycle Chalao! is a franchisee model. 'Bicycle sharing is a very localized business,' says Raj. Cycle Chalao! would provide a toolkit and the brand to enable franchisees to set up operations in their own cities. Importantly, Raj still hopes to secure the big advertising contracts that would make the franchisee model eminently viable.

With government support, there is new hope but the challenges remain. This road ahead is daunting—a number of alternative bicycle-sharing operations in India have been tried and have failed—Delhi, Thane, all harbour graves of failed bicycle-sharing start-ups. Raj, with his success in North Mumbai, had an opportunity to vie for a massive contract with the city government in Mumbai. But that fell through, over disagreements. There is a large fund allocation—several crores—and the concept may still happen in Mumbai on a large scale, but there are issues to work through. And that takes time.

Raj had better luck with the neighbouring city of Pune—the Pune Municipal Corporation is backing the 'rent-a-bicycle' scheme in the city and ready to provide ₹3.5 crore out of the total project cost of ₹9 crore. The plan is to set up twenty-five cycle stations, and equip these with 300 bicycles. Raj believes, with his usual approach of 'jump in with both feet' that he can make Cycle Chalao! scale in a big way in Pune, even if his Mumbai expansion plans are on hold. 'We need a big corporate sponsor for advertising.' He grins.

As I take his leave, Raj is already back on the phone. With a phone call to one of his new hires, perhaps, or to an official from a city government, or a venture capitalist who wants to help him scale his venture globally or a potential large corporate advertiser for Cycle Chalao!?

Fast forward to August 2012, it's now two years since Raj has co-founded Cycle Chalao! with his colleague Jui and both of them have bootstrapped, raised finance, piloted projects, reached the highest levels of advocacy amongst the public authorities, created global partnerships and have gained detailed knowledge of the bicycle-sharing world! But all these things did not help to get the first-ever government contract at Pune city going. The political class being a major deterrent, there was a deep flaw in the business model as well.

'There are two kinds of business models we've seen in bicycle-sharing world. We call them the European style and the Chinese style. The European style means the model where the revenues are significantly drawn from the outdoor advertising aka corporate sponsorships. The Chinese style is where the local public authority considers the bicycle-sharing project as one of the important public infrastructure projects and hence has greater ownership, which means they contract a private party for the model without making it dependent on the outdoor advertisement revenue. The reason being the pricing and volume of outdoor advertising are very different and are not conducive to supporting the bicycle-sharing sustenance. While there are several think tanks and transport expert institutions along with us, I feel all of us have done a mistake by advocating the European-style model in India . . . So here we are now with a government contract which essentially says they will support the bicycle-sharing systems if we make money from outdoor advertisements! We spent nearly six months running and reaching out to more than ninety private corporations in India and could not convince one of them to get on board in supporting the initiative. It was not about the financial returns; corporations here spend—read waste—a lot of money on marketing and advertising with little ROI [return on investment] but there were issues like dependence on the government, our start-up timing and the contractual nature of the outdoor ads. Adding to our problems is the requirement of bank guarantees for getting even a rupee from the government, something we failed to arrange. This meant for us to get three and a half crore from the government, we needed to produce bank guarantees of three and a half crore! This just does not make sense for a start-up in the PPP [public–private partnership] model. Thus you see all the companies contracting with government are never start-ups or smaller companies; hence all our government projects lose out on the benefits of contracting a small company in PPP models!

'We worked with some of the biggest private corporations including the world's leading investment companies but nothing paid off within the deadlines we had to commit to the government. Finally, we went to the government, told the authorities everything and asked for help. Of course they couldn't help and we finally decided to shut down!

'It took months to think through various strategies; we could have easily done several smaller projects but we believe intensely that successful bicycle sharing is the one with thousands of bicycle stations in our cities, not tens or hundreds! And we for one strongly believed in scale and if this was not possible, we did not want to carry on. By this time we had also exhausted our cash and had had long discussions with our investors. It was a collective decision to call it a day. We were amazed at the way we were supported by India Cycle Service, especially Mr Prabhat Agarwal, whom I would consider as a role model to all those who have a desire to mentor start-ups in India. He not only understood the business but had a very powerful understanding of myself and my co-founder!

'All the mentors in my life have always pushed me to be myself! People ask us about the number of employees we have, to judge our strength, but when they hear about the network of our advisers and mentors, they get stunned and wish they had had such support! What more can a start-up social entrepreneur ask for more than a mentor who understands you and pushes you to get clarity on the purpose of your life rather than simply making money! Three such individuals who will always be considered as my gurus are Mr Prabhat Agarwal, Dr Meena Galliara and Ms Pooja Warier. I love them as much as my family and have grown to what I am today because of them!

'We feel very happy to have friends from hundreds of cities and institutions and we hope to keep this relationship going in our next *big* entrepreneurial venture. Among other things, we feel victorious to know that the urban development ministry, Government of India, has released a bicycle-sharing toolkit with emphasis on the business model we have advocated so far and some other cities have *now* modified and announced contracts in the way we have actively pursued.

'The conclusion of our entire research, piloting, advocacy and working with government contracts is that the bicycle-sharing systems, if they are to be successful in India, have to be fully sponsored by the public authorities, wherein the private corporations shall act as contractors to provide construction, operations and maintenance alone.

'We accept our failure to carry on and wish to acknowledge the higher understanding of businesses, impact investments, working of public authorities and social-entrepreneurial landscape in India, all thanks to the fantastic support from our investors, mentors, advisers, interns, volunteers and incubating institutions with special thanks to the team at India Cycle Service!

'Just when Pooja Warier came to know about our decision to shut down Cycle Chalao! she immediately informed me about the expansion plans of UnLtd India. UnLtd India is searching for affiliates to replicate the model in other states and the suggestion came from across the family and mentors and from within to understand this opportunity. Having thought over it for some time, I am simply excited about the prospects of running an UnLtd India in Andhra Pradesh! The opportunity is still in process and I would get this opportunity only if I pass the selection process. While I am working on this opportunity now, I am also doing some winding-up tasks

and am on a break for several months—kind of a sabbatical—
before I start with my next social-entrepreneurial calling.

'I am happy and fortunate to have had such immense
experience and support. It's just a matter of time—I believe I
will be doing bigger and better public service.'

## What's New?

When we ask Raj about the things that have happened since
we last touched base, he says he has some fantastic updates!

'As I closed Cycle Chalao! in 2012 I should admit I was
not only confused about my own entrepreneurial ability once
again but also overwhelmed with the "job offers" from some
reputed social enterprises. I took a three-month break from
my routine and went on to study some books which I always
wanted to, including reading the whole text of the *Arthashastra*
by Kautilya.'

He deliberated over Pooja Warier's suggestion, then finally
took the plunge and applied for starting UnLtd Hyderabad
which will become a launch pad for social entrepreneurs in
Andhra Pradesh. He says, 'It is very difficult to find a higher
sense of fulfilment for an entrepreneur than in supporting the
start-up journey of others. Launching UnLtd Hyderabad so
I could do just that was the best decision I could have made
in this phase of my life. Having experienced first hand the
power of incubation support, I believe it is most effective when
offered close to home.' With the support and experience of
UnLtd India, he is thrilled to help accelerate the growth of
social entrepreneurs in Andhra Pradesh!

He has moved from Mumbai to Andhra Pradesh and made a new home. Since February 2013, when he started the research and prep work for launching UnLtd Hyderabad, every single day has been overwhelming, with challenges as well as opportunities to make change happen. 'On the personal front I find much more time now to spend with my family, special ones and a lot of friends, while I cautiously craft my work–life balance with my experience of running a social venture over the last three years.

'Establishing UnLtd Hyderabad has been extraordinarily fulfilling, especially the support from people at UnLtd India, like Sarah Allen who looks after expansion, helped a lot.' The increased participation of the larger community in supporting social entrepreneurs in Hyderabad is a sure sign of their early success in their model in the field. This is demonstrated by the fact that 200 people turned up to a social-entrepreneurial networking event they held in Hyderabad in March 2013. 'Right now we are a four-member team working on providing incubation support to ten highly exceptional social entrepreneurs from Andhra Pradesh, selected out of a pool of over fifty applicants. I have personally walked over 100 kilometres in the remotest part of Andhra Pradesh in my quest to understand the complex development challenges.

'I can say that the toughest of the decisions I have taken so far in the most chaotic situations in life have always led to the best of times in my entrepreneurial journey. I am now on a mission to provide support to at least 100 social entrepreneurs across Andhra Pradesh by way of our incubation services in the next three to five years.' He feels they have just touched a corner of a large canvas of ecosystem that is yet to emerge in Andhra Pradesh for social entrepreneurs. 'It's just a matter of time before the government and all of the corporate sector participates in building this ecosystem.'

# 8

# BLISS!

SABA GUL

Saba Gul is an engineer turned entrepreneur with a passion for female education and empowerment. Born and brought up in Pakistan, she did her graduation and postgraduation from the prestigious Massachusetts Institute of Technology (MIT). She returned to Pakistan and founded Business and Life Skills School (BLISS), which is dedicated to lifting adolescent girls and their families out of poverty through education and entrepreneurship. BLISS helps girls who have dropped out of school to get their education and become financially independent. The BLISS model is based on getting girls back to school, turning classwork into income and providing compensation to girls for the time spent in school and away from labour. BLISS supplements the regular English, Urdu, science and maths curriculum with a one-hour skills class and lessons in entrepreneurship. The girls are trained to create, design and market beautiful, socially conscious handbags. These bags are then sold and generate profit. These profits not only fund their education but also provide savings for the community.

SABA GUL was born in Karachi, Pakistan, and spent most of her childhood in Abbottabad and Lahore. Her family was distinctly upper middle class, with both parents being successful career professionals in Pakistan. Her father started his career in the Pakistan Navy, then turned entrepreneur and thereafter held several senior management and board-level positions in large multinational corporations. Her mother was a gynaecologist with a distinctive career, who still did her best to serve the underprivileged patients who came to her, often treating them free of cost.

Saba was the second of four children. Right from an early age, she was very competitive and an extremely bright student—from the first year she entered school to the day of graduation, she was always the top ranker. 'It could not have been any other way,' says Saba with a smile. 'I took great pride in being the best.'

A somewhat strange occurrence was the fashion of her entry into school: she repeated first grade three times. Having been enrolled in the first grade at the exceptionally young age of two, the school thought it best to let her age catch up with her class. 'At the time, I had no idea I was being made to repeat. Perhaps I would be three years ahead in my life now if they hadn't noticed my age. Ha ha!'

'My father always wanted me to take up medicine,' she

recollects. 'But I had the freedom to explore, to read, to try different things. I had a very comfortable childhood . . . I remember, my dream in those days was to be left for the whole day at the British Council Library. I loved the smell of books, old and new. I would devour all kinds of books there. My favourite author at the time was Enid Blyton . . . the only thing I was upset with was they only allowed me to check out four books at a time!'

All those Enid Blyton books—The Famous Five, The Secret Seven and the like—and it was therefore no surprise that the young Saba decided that her career ahead lay as a detective!

While her elder sister went to medical school, she grew close to her two younger brothers, and the three of them would spend hours doing typical childhood things: playing video games for hours, playing cricket, which Saba was not particularly good at!

Having eventually grown out of her Famous-Five detective phase, she enrolled, on the recommendation of her father, for pre-med, with a clear path ahead to become a doctor, like her mother and elder sister. But, meanwhile, computers had caught the fancy of young Saba—this was the '90s, the age when the field was growing rapidly and *anything* seemed possible. 'At the very last minute, without telling my father, I applied for a bachelor's degree in computer science, at MIT, no less.' There was no preparation, no counselling—there was no time!

Having started the process late, in September, Saba scrambled to fill in her application—statement of purpose and the works—by the December deadline.

'Miraculously,' she smiles, 'I got in . . . I was alone at home when I received the news, and I was jumping up and down on the bed in happiness.'

Computer science (CS) at the Massachusetts Institute of Technology. Wow!

This was the Mecca of computer science, where many of the technologies that we take for granted today emerged from, and where every day new research and innovation is taking the field even farther.

Naturally, her family was pleasantly surprised and very excited.

'They were very supportive. My mother was probably more excited than I was, if that was possible!' She remembers, 'Before I knew it, it was time to leave home, leave Pakistan . . . and go to the United States of America, to this new life . . .'

A completely new phase in life was about to start for Saba.

'You know what? My childhood ended just then, at that moment . . . I went to MIT . . . and lost my innocence!' She laughs.

Saba had travelled some parts of the Middle East with her parents before but Boston and MIT were a completely novel experience.

'The first thing I remember is how international everything was. I mean my class of ninety-one had only eleven American students and eighty internationals—from all over the world: Zimbabwe, Nigeria, Sweden . . . It was a very far cry from Lahore, 90 per cent Punjabi, where everyone followed the same religion, thought in similar ways . . . MIT was like this big playground, this fantasy land . . .'

After the initial excitement had subsided, interacting with

this truly international group made her question some of the things she had always believed in.

'For instance, take the notion of "fact". Like things one is taught at school—say the history of the times of Pakistan and India's experience. I realized that my Indian friends at MIT and I were looking back at the same piece of time but had been taught very different versions of history. I watched Attenborough's *Gandhi* movie and was really surprised at my Indian friend's perception of Jinnah. In Pakistan, he is viewed as a father, a hero. But to Indians, I realized, he is an instigator of the Partition, a troublemaker! Similarly, there are very different versions of "facts" on each side of the India–Pakistan wars . . .'

Discussing these issues in the rarefied, intellectual air of Cambridge, amongst friends, including those from across the border, made Saba realize that history is subjective and depends on the narrator, the writer. These discussions were interspersed in between the hectic bursts of activity that MIT is famous— or rather, infamous!—for: classes, projects, assignments and more, until you can hardly keep up. The competition and the pressure were legendary. At times, there was no time to do anything but run and try to keep pace with everything—no time for friends or family.

'You know, overall, I really had a fantastic time there. It made me who I am. But I would say, at the time, it was a love-hate relationship. We used to have this acronym: IHTFP. Depending on the time of day, it could stand for "I have truly found paradise" or "I hate this fucking place".'

Like many very smart people before her, Saba realized that at MIT she could be guaranteed to find someone even smarter!

To someone who had never stood anything but first in class, it was quite a humbling experience to get her first-ever C in physics, despite putting in the full quota of hard work. Saba made friends, worked hard and lived the undergrad life in Cambridge.

'There is, like, a rule . . . consider three things—studies, friends, sleep. Now pick one, at most two! That's what MIT demands from you . . .'

Saba was an adventurous freshman at MIT.

'I remember getting into trouble with the MIT campus police because my friends and I kept breaking into the under-construction building areas for fun.' She laughs. 'I learnt many things outside the classroom, like how to sail—I still have a sailing licence and loved sailing on the Charles River.'

Saba interned at tech start-ups in the Silicon Valley and in the Boston area, like many of her CS peers. This was her first real work experience, her first impression of the 'real world'.

She loved the start-up culture—where even a young intern like her was given difficult and challenging problems to solve and expected to come up with solutions for the team, where there was little hierarchy and everything was lean, fast and effective.

'It was exciting for me! Even as an intern, I interfaced with experienced developers, who took me seriously, where my feedback was valued, where critical thinking was encouraged. And the amazing thing was that even for really big decisions, there were four guys in a room and bam, done, decision taken! No bureaucracy . . .'

So did she think she could stay on and make a career in a

tech start-up? Perhaps follow the well-trodden path of people from the subcontinent who came, learnt and started the next big thing of their own in the land of opportunity?

'Well, to be honest, I was, despite the amazing work culture, somewhat disillusioned . . . I really did not know what I would be doing in my life, but I was not motivated by developing technology, at least not the kind that I was developing during my internship. My job was writing code, checking it and rewriting it. I stayed up nights, missed meals doing it—I was dedicated and competitive. But I think that was just me being me—being competitive and very good at things. But I did not love the code. It did not light my fire at all . . .'

One summer, she got a job in India but she did not get the visa and so never went. In her senior year, she got her first 'non-tech' work opportunity—an assignment in Sri Lanka, building databases for an organization called Saryabodiya. This was a big organization that was, after the tsunami, tracking information about people affected by the disaster. Her next project was also interesting—it was assembling solar-lighting kits for a European organization called Light up the World. 'We installed the lighting systems in refugee camps at Trincomalee, along the eastern coast of Sri Lanka.'

In Sri Lanka, Saba was experiencing something else. In Pakistan her childhood had been upper middle class, completely sheltered—she had never travelled by public transport, never talked to street vendors. Apart from the economic divide, the situation was different, being a girl in Pakistan. Sri Lanka had the same 'developing-country' feel—there were differences but many similarities. But here, Saba was on her own, face-to-face with reality, playing cricket in the sand with village children, getting on public buses that had barely any place to stand—if you lifted your foot, there was no place to put it down again!

Trincomalee was a life-changing experience for Saba. 'I was amazed and touched by random acts of everyday kindness shown by the poor—they hardly had enough to feed themselves, but never failed to greet me as their guest with tea and biscuits.'

Saba was in Sri Lanka for three months, with three other girls from MIT. One of them, Alia Whitney, went on to found in Sri Lanka the NGO Emerge Global that helps rape and abuse victims reintegrate into society.

'Sri Lanka affected me profoundly. After that, I decided I wanted to travel, to see the world . . . I didn't want to be in the US or in Pakistan . . .'

She had a stint as a research intern at the National Centre for Scientific Research in France.

Next, Saba spent a summer in Ethiopia, teaching computer science at the Addis Ababa University. It was a very different culture—Saba had again a great summer, a very enriching experience.

Despite these experiences from all around the world, at the time when she had to make her career choice, as she graduated with a bachelor's degree in computer science from MIT, she still hesitated in following her heart. 'I still wanted to give my CS degree from MIT a chance . . . so I joined Oracle in San Francisco . . .' Beginning the fall of 2006, she worked there for one year but was not particularly happy or engaged. 'San Francisco is a great city to live in, my colleagues at Oracle were fantastic, but I just didn't want to get up in the morning and do the work I was doing . . . I found myself discussing this with my colleagues—about how depressing it was that people would spend more than a third of their lives doing work that they did not enjoy. I mean—what is the point?'

Saba did not have an idea what she would do next—perhaps a PhD? Perhaps academia might be better suited to her, more exciting?

Seeking answers, Saba went back to MIT, to do her master's. While her area of expertise was artificial intelligence, she still got a chance to work on very different projects with Professor Amy Smith at the D-Lab. This was a lab that had a track record of developing appropriate technology suited for conditions in the developing world.

'I have tremendous respect for Professor Amy Smith—to dedicate your entire life to this is amazing and very useful to the world,' Saba gushes. She was also infected now by the entrepreneurial culture of the place. 'I saw the MIT $100K ideas competition. This was—and is!—very big. I had an idea that I thought might really help people, so I made a plan and put it in . . .'

This was the plan for what was to become BLISS.

Meanwhile, she decided to seek out a job in the development sector in the US. This was tougher than she had imagined. She spoke to many people, sought out sponsorship.

'It is unbelievable how difficult it is for a young non-American to get this kind of job,' she says. 'Either you need a lot of experience, or you need to be an American citizen—it was very frustrating. I tried to get into the Peace Corps . . .

everything! But I did not have any contacts anywhere, and nothing worked out at any of the places I applied to.'

So eventually, Saba ended up opting for a different track—she took up a role at Thomson Reuters. This was a job that utilized her MIT computer science skill set to the fullest. 'This was really amazing. They had specifically created a role for me. I was an architect, sitting between the developer and the business people. I was designing the software—it was a great job. And a six-figure salary to match!'

Perhaps in an alternate universe, Saba would have continued at this job.

But in the background, another story was being born: BLISS.

The plan that Saba had made and submitted in 2009 at the MIT $100K Entrepreneurship Competition had won a not insignificant amount of US$5000 in prize money. Using this, she had put the first part of her plan into action, as a pilot project in Pakistan.

The idea's origins lay in a talk by Arti Pandey at MIT. Arti was the co-founder of Barakat—an organization that was starting schools all over Afghanistan, trying to provide education for the thousands of refugees all over the country. Saba heard from her, the story of Azaada Khan—an Afghan girl who was so fed up with being denied education as a girl that she dressed up as a boy and tried to get her fundamental right. She called herself 'Azaad' and disguised herself as a boy for twelve years just so that she could attend school. Under the Taliban regime, this was a severely punishable crime.

'I was very moved. There are girls like Azaada Khan from

Afghanistan, from Pakistan, who have to fight so hard their whole lives. They have to hide their gender; they have their fathers killed off . . .'

Saba wanted to meet Azaada Khan. She went to Afghanistan in the winter of 2009, and did just that. She was determined to do something to improve things. In January 2009, she visited many marginalized communities, in remote parts of the country. 'Girls there have no opportunities. They are stuck in a vicious circle . . . of illiteracy, poverty . . . There is no way out. In the remote community I visited, they spoke only their own local dialect. They did not even speak Urdu; they had no idea of what was happening in the world; they had no education, no access to proper nutrition or basic vaccination. In Pakistan, things were bad but this was ridiculous here. They had no education; none of them had ever been outside or even had any hope of doing so. For instance, there was only one seat allocated for the entire region in the medical college in Punjab! There was no right to dream of a different life—nothing! I saw girls working long hours at carpet looms, working fourteen hours a day. There was no option of school, no question at all! These girls and their families have been stuck in this vicious cycle for generations. They are illiterate because they are poor and they are poor because they are illiterate . . .'

The saddest thing Saba saw was girls dropping out of school at the age of twelve, thirteen, fourteen. 'Then they would marry and have kids. The end . . .'

What struck Saba the most was the stark contrast in the opportunities that she herself had had in life to those which these girls had.

Saba started thinking of ways in which she could keep girls from dropping out.

The basic thing, she realized, was to convince their families that the girls were better off in school than out of it. She had to find a way to make school pay. She had to find a pragmatic approach that balanced the girl's learning needs and the pressing economic concerns of her parents, often under immense pressure to put the girl to work to supplement their daily wage.

It is a difficult problem, and Saba was very keen to find a practical solution. Education for girls is the best long-term investment anyone could ever make—but in the absence of any practical solutions, many lives were being wasted.

The tangible idea that eventually became Business and Life Skills School came from the community. What if one could learn useful skills in school that could be instantly monetized? Along with the regular classes, what if there were more hands-on courses in embroidery, crafts and other skills that could be used to develop the girls' capacity to earn? To make products for sale, and become contributors to their families' incomes, in whatever small way? Make school a place for learning and earning both. Have a person affiliated to the school who would also help advise on designs and marketing and how to convert skills into a product that the rich urban markets would pay for. Make each girl an entrepreneur.

This was her business plan based on the rather pragmatic idea that won the MIT $100K ideas contest and helped Saba start the pilot with the prize money of US$5000.

'I remember we kicked off the pilot for BLISS in late

2009–early 2010. Just about the time I was joining Thomson Reuters in the US. It became very hectic for me—I spent all my lunch breaks doing things for BLISS, making phone calls. I spent all nights, weekends . . .'

She was getting encouragement and advice from her MIT friends. At the start, the core team consisted of herself; Elene Orphnidis, a friend from MIT; and Sana Kazmi, another MIT friend, who relocated to Pakistan, managing operations. 'Many people gave us their time when we were starting out and helped us. None of them are with us at present, but those early volunteers were great to have!'

Saba remembers setting up the pilot: 'I had an appointment with the principal of the local school, to pitch my idea. When I got out of the school, there were forty middle-aged men standing there, waiting for me. It was hugely intimidating. But I realized they were there to help! They gave ideas, their views, their inputs, on what we should do. The village elders were enthusiastic and supportive. "Send your daughters to school and let them make money too!" they said. Their support was vital in getting the buy-in of the community . . .'

Using the school as her first base and the US$5000 in prize money from MIT, she started BLISS with the first batch of girl students. They had to train teachers, include additional courses in life skills and entrepreneurship in the everyday classes.

'We made mistakes, of course. We were learning by doing, learning on the ground. But we were learning . . .'

Saba soon realized she would have to choose—her job at Thomson Reuters or BLISS. She was enjoying her work in the US, designing software for the news giant. However, it was easy to make the decision once she saw the results of the BLISS pilot: beautiful bags made by her girls, happy girls. The choice was made. She resigned from her job in January 2011 and now could focus full-time on her social venture.

'Things were happening. The initial pilot results were promising—the girls were making bags, and the products were rather nice. Most importantly, the girls were all in school! Maryam Tahir Khan, a designer, had joined us in 2010. We were also getting a lot of visibility—I was at a dinner where Hillary Clinton and the US state department gave us recognition—they called us "young change makers". It was really good for us . . . Amongst other things, it really helped at home. My father was impressed. He told me, "So you are having dinners with Hillary now! Tell me more about what you are up to . . ."'

The BLISS model has evolved only slightly over time. The central premise is to augment schools, not to replace them. To supplement the education they provide with more practical training that will help the girls and their families directly, in the short term.

'I know much more about these things than I knew back then,' says Saba with a smile, talking about quality management systems at BLISS. 'When we started, despite the promise of some very nice bags made by the initial batch, there was a long way to go. When I compare their quality, the first batch of products was terrible! It was shameful; we had to improve if we were to stay sustainable.

'Our model is—we teach and help the girls make embroidery. The bags come from a professional bag maker, on to which the girls stitch their designs. It took us a while to find good-quality bag makers and then even longer to enforce our standards of design and quality on their work output. Initially, Sana Kazmi—an artist—was handling operations and her idea of quality was different from mine. I wasn't happy with our initial quality at all . . . The only way to get quality is to be there, on the ground. There is no substitute for that. That's one of the reasons I knew I had to be in this full-time. You can't delegate things. I realized that I had to do this myself; I couldn't tell others to do this from the US. This was *my* job.'

Saba worked voraciously and aggressively, finding high-quality reliable bag makers in Lahore, convincing them to become suppliers and then managing the continuing battle of quality control.

She had also hired Abdur Rehman, a fifteen-year veteran from Arti Pandey's operation, Barakat, as her right-hand man. His nous on the ground helped!

There were also simple but high-impact learning from being on the ground.

'For instance, we had initially not thought of involving the mothers. They were not allowed in school. But we soon learnt that making them a part of the process actually improves outcomes; more girls stay and learn once their mothers are involved at school also. So now we have a process by which mothers are at school, helping their daughters . . . After all, if the mothers want to be there, why should we stop them?'

Saba faced many a challenge getting everything up and running.

Firstly, for the embroidery, they needed clean cloth. 'We had constant communication problems with our suppliers. I said, "You can't keep sending us dirty cloth; we need to do *chaapa* on the *kapda*, then the embroidery." But I still kept getting dirty cloth and, inevitably, in those early days, I was the one spending hours scrubbing out the dirt in the cloth,' recollects Saba. 'In those moments, I often asked myself—"Saba, look at yourself, what are you doing here?"'

A big problem was money. 'Always, we had no money!' She laughs.

Abdur Rehman, her key operations man on the ground, was not getting paid; the teachers were due back pay for the work because BLISS was always short of funds. The US$5000 from the MIT prize money had long gone since the pilot. She had then also invested all her personal savings into the project.

'I would love to do this but the teachers are getting frustrated. They are poor, they have families . . . if you don't pay them, this will fail,' advised Abdur Rehman.

This was a wake-up call for Saba.

'Project managers and teachers need to be paid. Only then will they take their jobs seriously. This is the only way to make them accountable.'

Moving quickly, she scrambled to raise funding. She put in place a strong incentive system for suppliers, rewarding clean-fabric delivery and resolutely penalizing substandard material. She put in place a formal salary structure. BLISS was now becoming a 'serious' organization, dragged along by Saba towards quality and accountability.

'Quality was not a choice for us,' says Saba. 'It was do or

die. Consider who buys the bags from us—a wealthy person in a city in Pakistan or US or Europe. They are paying US$100 or more for a bag. They are not going to accept any blemish, any bad marks on the bag. There was no option of having glue visible, or a buckle placed in the wrong place. It had to be perfect!'

The core team, apart from Abdur Rehman, consisted of three enterprising women. Maryam Tahir Khan, the designer and an art school graduate with an exceptionally creative mind; Aisha Navaz, an MBA with a strong background in the development sector, microfinance and economics; and, lastly, Saba herself.

It is tough for women to do business in Pakistan.

'You see, it was the *kaarigars*—people who make leather, buckles, and so on—whom we had to deal with on a day-to-day basis. If you are a woman, they don't take you seriously. They will overcharge you because they think you don't know what you are doing.'

Saba took along Abdur Rehman to help with the negotiations. 'You have to lay down the law. "This is how it is going to work", you must say, and stick with it!' She grins.

Saba struggled with quality issues on a daily basis. She also realized that the biggest challenge was getting a non-profit organization to run with the efficiency of a profit-making business. She used all her learning, all the lessons learnt in her stints in Silicon Valley and Route 128 and tried to make BLISS work seamlessly, delivering high-quality output.

'This is the way to go, you know. You have to be efficient, even if you are a non-profit concern. Perhaps especially if you are a non-profit . . . People ask me, "What is your 'plan'?" Here's what I think—there are more than 600 million [60 crore] girls in the developing world we can impact. Why should I pick a number and limit myself to those? What about the rest? I want to impact everyone!'

BLISS is increasing its coverage school by school. They are collaborating with the CARE foundation, which runs about a hundred schools, and with TCF, another large organization running schools.

'As we expand and scale, the skill and product mix may change. But we expect to have a focus on the luxury product market, the high-fashion industry. There is so much demand there . . . Imagine all that money going straight to these girls.'

Apart from handbags, BLISS now also makes custom pouches for top-of-the-line jewellery (custom gemstones or other jewels made by top designers, items that often retail at more than US$10,000). Saba is very proud of the pouch designs—they are hers!

'It is a promising business. The customer places an order and we produce it on demand. There is no inventory. The pouch is something the girls can stitch themselves, unlike the handbags. The shorter the value chain, the better it is . . .'

Apart from being an Unreasonable Fellow, 2011, Saba is also a StartingBloc Fellow, 2011. In addition to her work being recently recognized by the US Department of State via the dinner invitation from Secretary Hillary Clinton, BLISS has been featured by NBC News, *MIT Technology Review*, *Providence Business News*, the *Express*, the *Tribune* and various other publications.

The mission of BLISS remains strong—to create a viable livelihood for girls and also make sure they don't miss out on education. The girls don't work full-time but have a full curriculum in school that they go through. But the BLISS system is practical—it provides the incentive for both girls and parents to want the girls to be in school, to complete their education.

Saba has great plans for the future, to expand the BLISS model beyond Pakistan and Afghanistan, to India and Bangladesh, as well as African nations that suffer from the same vicious cycle.

'The more products we can make, the more girls we can educate and train and keep in school . . .' It is a virtuous cycle. BLISS also has a business and financial literacy curriculum that it wants to expand, to enable more girls with tools and training to launch their own handicrafts microenterprises. Saba is also very cognizant of the pitfalls of depending on revenue streams from only one product line and has plans to expand into other segments. She is also aggressively building up a list of retailers who would stock, showcase and promote her products in major cities in the world. The proceeds from the sales are fed back into the BLISS engine—education and community development, funding another batch of girls.

It is an interesting model, for sure!

The ultimate vision is of *no girl left behind*, to have every girl empowered to determine her own destiny in life.

'I do this work from the heart. It is worth my time. It drives me,' she says.

## What's New?

As 2013 begins, Saba recalls how the past year has been: '2012 was about progress and breakthroughs. Our top five milestones were: (1) securing our first major investment, which will allow us to grow by four times in 2013; (2) hiring our first paid/full-time team members; (3) selling our products in thirty cities around the world with demand surpassing my wildest expectations, and customer testimonials that gave me goosebumps; (4) scaling to our second community of low-income women (we will be starting a third in March); (5) engaging a network of global brand ambassadors that include Pulitzer-Prize winners and top executives at Fortune 500 companies. Along the way, we launched our new website, set up our online shop with three-day delivery to every corner of the world, did our first trunk show in the US, got coverage in the media like *Vogue* Magazine and featured our products at places like London Fashion Week and at fashion shows in New York.

'But what I am most proud of is the fact that we have created incomes for ninety marginalized girls and women, most of whom had never before felt the dignity of earning their own money. The smiles I see on these women's faces—smiles that come from choice and opportunity—are my greatest reward. At every milestone we meet, I feel grateful for the courage to have taken the plunge a year and a half ago by quitting my job in the US and moving to Pakistan.

'At the same time, 2012 was a year of trials and tribulations for BLISS. We had to shut down operations at our first community in Attock because of security concerns, and move to a new community near Lahore. It was the most difficult decision I have made since BLISS was conceived—one that kept me up nights and really tested my wits. The Attock girls were my inspiration for the work I do. I knew each of them by name; I knew their stories; I had seen them transform—week by week, month by month—into confident young girls who could now dare to dream. I can never forget their innocent, hopeful faces and I can never thank them enough for what they taught me about resilience and optimism. In the end, I chose the path I felt was best for the organization and that allowed us to continue spreading our work and mission without jeopardizing the safety of our team.

'Also this year, to the disappointment of our customers, we were unable to launch any new collections and continued to sell our 2011 line. While we experimented with various new designs, we struggled to establish a cohesive design narrative and to put our ideas into commercial production. Related to this was the challenge of defining a brand identity that could guide our future products. The good news is that we have several exciting new products, designs and ideas brewing; the first quarter of 2013 will bring many of these to life!

'We also struggled to build the team, which meant we were unable to scale operations fast enough to meet the demand for our products. At times, some of our customers had to wait weeks, even months, for their orders to be delivered. Hiring has been my biggest lesson for 2012. Without the right people, we are as good as dead. Having made a couple of crucial hiring mistakes this past year, I learnt that the single-most important trait in a great hire is that they be fit for the start-up culture and for the values of the organization. I wrote a post on NextBillion in October sharing these lessons, which was selected by the editors as one of the best posts of 2012 and republished in December.

'But hidden in each of these challenges was an opportunity, a chance to create systems and processes within the organization that will be effective and replicable. At the end of it all, we're bigger, stronger and more ready to tackle the problems we set out to solve when we launched in 2011.

'Lastly, 2012 was about turning points—we went from being a non-profit to a for-profit. I'm thrilled about this shift and the direction it's steered us in. While our social mission of boosting incomes at the bottom of the pyramid remains unchanged, I believe being a for-profit will allow us to grow faster, become more competitive, as well as attract the right talent and investors.

'I also want to give you a glimpse into what lies ahead for us. 2013 will see BLISS launching two new product lines, scaling its impact to 200 women across Punjab, and hiring three new team members. We're also in the midst of rebranding and restructuring the organization to build an ethical fashion label that can compete in any market. Stay tuned for a major announcement on this front in the first quarter of 2013!

'I have never been more full of excitement, hope and inspiration for BLISS and what the coming year will bring. I believe that consumers worldwide now want to know that their dollars are creating positive change—that, at the very least, the products they buy are not making the planet worse off. My vision is to create breathtakingly beautiful products that offer dignity, opportunity and growth to those living at the bottom of the pyramid. The fashion/apparel industry is the second-largest industry in the world, and employs more than 250 million people . . . 75 per cent of whom live in the developing world. This industry is uniquely placed to create large impact that can alleviate poverty—yet this very industry is ranked the second-worst in the world (up there with the oil industry) for environmental and social abuse. I dream of changing these statistics.'

# 9

# MAKING THE WORLD A BETTER PLACE

## LUIS DUARTE

Luis Duarte is the founder of YoReciclo, a company which offers consulting services to develop customized recycling solutions for institutions to reduce their waste, embrace and understand recycling, and fulfil certifications/law requirements.

YoReciclo designs and implements recycling solutions for various institutions. It educates, trains, and collects and turns recyclable materials into raw materials that can then be sold. By doing this, they create jobs and monitor the environmental impact per customer.

The company is increasing cities' recycling rates and diverting useful waste to reduce pollution and indiscriminate extraction of natural resources by educating/training people and by filling up the missing links within the recycling chain in Mexico.

LUIS WAS born in 1981 in a small city in Mexico, called Chihuahua, in a very warm and loving family. He was the middle child to his parents—Francesco and Imelda. He has an elder brother, whose name is also Francesco, and a younger sister, Arlee, who, Luis fondly says, has a beautiful smile.

An incident, very early on in his life, shaped him as a person. Since his early childhood, he was involved with La Salle School, which is a Catholic school. By the time he was eleven, someone invited him to the missions. Since all his friends were going for the missions, he decided to take part too. They became missionaries. They prepared the material and gathered sponsorships to take building materials to rural communities. The missions had a huge impact on Luis.

'I think that experience shaped who I am right now. Going into these rural communities, I went as a cool kid, to teach people how to do things. But something totally different happened. All those people were so incredibly amazing. As soon as we went to the villages, they would give us all they had. Just because they knew we came to help them and they appreciated it. At the end, we were the ones being helped!'

After that first time, Luis spent thirteen years doing the same. He visited about 70 per cent of the rural communities in Chihuahua. The place that they went to is called La Sierra Tarahumara (Tarahumaras are the indigenous people in

Chihuahua), Chihuahua. Luis felt amazing going there and every time he got an opportunity to visit, he would. Later, he would return feeling 'super good' as he puts it.

Luis' dad, Francesco, is a civil engineer, who worked for a large cement company in Chihuahua. Upon reaching the executive level, he decided to quit and start his own business. That's where Luis gets the entrepreneurial genes from! His mother was a full-time homemaker, which Luis especially loved, since she was always there for him when he needed her. Theirs is a typical Mexican family—the father being the breadwinner and the mother staying at home.

'In Mexico, the value of families is very strong. So we had gatherings with cousins, celebrations of festivals—all those things that families do together. My love for music comes from my grandfather—who is an amazing cello player. I like singing and playing the guitar!'

As soon as he finished high school, Luis went to Monterrey. He knew there were better opportunities outside Chihuahua. In Monterrey, Luis chose to study mechanical engineering, since he had always had an interest in maths and physics. He had dreamt of becoming an engineer since he was a child and the path was set.

He pursued mechanical engineering from Tec of Monterrey, Mexico—which is one of the largest private systems of schools in the world. In the first years, Luis tried to keep up with the missions in Chihuahua, but it was too difficult, because of the distance; it's about an eight-hour drive.

In the second year of his engineering studies, he met Luis Daniel (who later became his partner). He was from La Salle, too, and had gone to the missions. They were together in the entrepreneurship class. They created a very simple product, which helped with hygiene, the process of which was so simple that they decided to provide jobs to people.

The product was very basic—paper toilet seat covers. It is a disposable piece of paper shaped like a toilet seat and can be placed on the seat to protect the user from germs that may be resting on the seat by creating a protective barrier. It is usually used when using a public toilet.

'In Mexico, that didn't exist. What we did was—we bought one of these boxes, with tonnes of such paper cuts and made sets of six. We then sold these packets to mothers and disabled people. The response was very good.'

It was a school project, which they won and got a scholarship to go to Tulane University, New Orleans. A professor there, Sidney Pulitzer, suggested to them that they go back to Mexico and restart that business. They took his suggestion and started their business, with $50,000, which they had received as prize money for the competition.

The company grew pretty well. They started exporting the product to Columbia and Guatemala. Their customers grew in number. They reached out to institutions, which were taking care of handicapped and disabled people and took permission to create the product in their workshops, for which they paid the participants. The people participated excitedly, because they did not usually get paid in workshops and the institutions were happy too.

'Our company was providing job opportunities to people with disabilities. It made me feel good about what we were doing.'

Luis' father did not like him drifting away from education, by getting involved in making money. Their business was doing okay—they were making profits and their expenses were taken care of. Luis was only nineteen and worked on weekends to keep this business going. He sometimes missed classes during the weekdays too—a fact his father did not approve of.

So Luis decided to stop working the operations section of the company and stay just a board member, to lessen his involvement in running the company.

He continued his studies, eventually falling in love with Germany and taking German classes. He was very fond of BMW cars and wanted to work for the company. For a student-exchange programme, he went to Germany for three months, during a summer. He travelled around nineteen different cities there and enjoyed himself.

After coming back, he closed the company; part of it was already sold. He completed his degree and then wanted to be a part of the labour force. His first job was in the plastic industry, for a company called Evco Plastics, which is based in Wisconsin but had a branch in Monterrey. He was in charge of operational efficiency and his job was to find out potential saving opportunities in the processes.

That was the first time Luis learnt about recycling because

Evco had 15 per cent scrap in their processes. They ground the scrap in fine grinders and sold the material to other plastic manufacturers. The company appreciated Luis and his work, for he was promoted to the title of project engineer, a job that he handled very well.

There was a mentor, who guided Luis through his decisions around that time. One of his bosses, Ruff Smith, was an American who had lived for over twenty years in Mexico. He was a close friend and mentor to the twenty-three-year-old Luis.

Around the time Luis took the promotion, there was another excellent opportunity to work in Chihuahua. They were looking for someone who had good management skills and also knew about the rural communities in Chihuahua. Luis was offered a position in the government. He wanted to go back to Chihuahua and the challenge in the position he was offered there was much bigger, which only added to his excitement to work there.

When he went for the interview, his boss-to-be said, 'Luis, tell me what you know!' Luis told him everything he knew about the plastic industry, rural communities and about his drive to learn. That was all he was asked in the interview; the job was his to take. He was twenty-four by then, and was leading sixty-year-old engineers in the State Health Department. He had a huge corner office there, which made him wonder what his job responsibility was.

When he asked his boss, he said, 'You'll figure it out!'

Later, Luis found out that he was in charge of two hundred clinics and twenty hospitals around the state. He needed to take care of all the electromechanical devices—elevators, heaters, biomedical devices such as X-rays—and the infrastructure of hospitals and clinics.

> 'When I asked my boss where my team was, he said to me, "You *are* the team." There were three people in the company that could help me, but all three of them wanted my position. So I was basically on my own!'

The first three months of working there were very difficult for Luis. The pay cheque he received there was lower than what he brought home from his first job, but he had taken this job up for the challenge that came with it. The impact that he could have was huge and that was what had attracted Luis to this job.

'I tried to define certain goals to reach in the time I was going to spend there. Because in Mexico there is a lot of corruption, but I was raised with values and bending rules is something I cannot do. So, I knew I was not going to be there for long because, even if I was put in a position where I could make decisions, I would always have had a lot of people above me, with a lot of power.'

The federal state wanted to have all the clinics and hospitals in federal standards to provide good health service. And Chihuahua was almost the last in the place. So Luis took that up as a challenge. They hired students, college grads, electrical engineers, civil engineers, et cetera, and built a team. There was a budget for that, so money was not an issue.

'We built a good team. In three or four months' time, the

engineers who didn't like me also joined the team because we were doing good work. In about a year and a half, almost all the hospitals and clinics were certified by federal standards. We were very pleased.'

When Luis was almost twelve months into this job, his boss decided to quit his job to build his own company. He was a very good man, but the man who replaced him was highly corrupt and reserved the contracts for his own family members and friends. Luis agreed to interview the people his boss 'suggested' along with the other applicants. But upon interviewing the men, Luis found that they had no knowledge or experience of the work they wanted to have the contracts for. They offered him money, to bribe their way into the jobs, which Luis declined without a moment's thought. His boss would get angry at him and Luis even started receiving threatening phone calls.

Luis was twenty-five, and did not want trouble in his life. He had anyway achieved the goals he had set for himself for his time in that company. So he quit his job and went to Germany again, with his savings. For three months, he worked small jobs such as bartending. He took a break from the regular day-to-day life and relaxed there. It was 2006, so Germany was hosting the FIFA World Cup and Luis got to watch a few Mexico games.

In the meantime, his mentor, Ruff Smith, suggested that Luis should go for an MBA. Taking his advice, Luis started preparing for GMAT and took the test. His score was good and, going back to Mexico, he started working on his applications. He applied to Babson College in Massachusetts and got in.

Because of his experience with work till then, he knew he wanted to be an entrepreneur and Babson was the place to be.

He was awarded a hundred per cent scholarship for the tuition fee, so he only needed to find means to sustain himself. Finding Massachusetts loan rates very attractive, he took a loan. He also had support from his family and friends, and they were always there if he needed help.

In the first year of his MBA, he got engaged. Before the second year began, he went back to Mexico to get married. He brought his wife to Massachusetts with him when he came back to join the school again.

In that year, he also met his current partner, who Luis likes to think as Finance Humanitarian Master. Hector had worked for Deloitte for five years in the MNA department, so he had a good understanding of finance. When Hector was a child, he had made a promise to himself to volunteer for a year in rural communities of Mexico before he got married. He quit Deloitte and went to Chiapas, which is in the south of Mexico. He volunteered there for a year, helping people. He went to Babson for an MBA after that, which was where Luis met him, in the year 2008.

They clicked instantly. Hector wanted to go back to Mexico and build his own company. It was very important for him to make an impact—either social or environmental. That was exactly what Luis wanted too, so they started creating a business plan together. At Babson, the professors pushed every student to find opportunities to create a sustainable business that also created an impact. Luis and Hector started looking at different statistics in different industries and found out that the recycling industry was just beginning to make its presence felt in Mexico.

Both Luis and Hector had been to rural communities and had personally experienced the lack of resources for the same. They had seen at first hand many people living in such communities who needed to walk long distances just to fetch water. They did not have lumber to keep themselves warm. Companies used to come into the communities and take everything away from them for their businesses.

'One beverage company once came in and fenced the only water well in the area to keep for themselves. The government had provided the company a concession. The people living in the area had to look for water elsewhere, usually places far away. They had to walk huge distances.'

'We wanted to do something to stop the extraction of natural resources. Some things just find their way to you. This was our calling.'

They found a recycling industry in Mexico. They knew that, on an average, the recycling rates in developed countries range from 30 to 50 per cent.

'In Mexico, the number was a meagre 3 per cent. Recycling rates in Latin America are close to nil—specifically in Mexico we recycle only 3.3 per cent while other countries recycle more than 50 per cent of their waste. News about trash suddenly appearing on our beaches, landfills running over capacity, et cetera, has made large and small corporations, governments and individuals now willing to change behaviour in these regions.'

Additionally, particularly in developing countries, more and more private and public institutions are looking for green certifications or even to fulfil requirements of environmental laws which governments have started to legislate and approve. This creates an important opportunity to increase recycling rates and impact the overall environment.

They saw an opportunity and wanted to bring up the number from three to thirty, maybe even fifty. They launched YoReciclo and started developing customized recycling programmes and solutions for schools and corporate offices. They provided educational material and gave lectures to the members of the institution to spread awareness about recycling and how it can make the world a better place.

So they started separating their waste, which YoReciclo collected from them. After every three months, they provided their customers with an environmental-impact certificate.

'YoReciclo strives to involve many individuals in recycling activities to achieve the goal: increasing recycling rates in developing countries to reduce global waste and the use of natural resources.'

With their lectures, educational material and certification, customers started reducing their waste disposal into landfills while saving costs and building their path to sustainability. They monitored what each customer was bringing in to recycle and then, every three months, provided them with an environmental-impact report summarizing the benefits of their efforts, which could be later marketed for brand purposes.

The way their business model yielded money was that they sorted out the materials and prepared them to be sold as raw materials. It is capital-intensive, so they needed to raise US$300,000 to start up. They needed to buy trucks to pick up the waste materials and machinery to convert them into raw materials that could be sold. They needed to rent a facility to operate from and hire employees.

They took a loan at a decent interest rate from the Family Bank to start the business. Luis and Hector had a fifty-fifty partnership in the company. Their idea worked; the company started flourishing. Manufacturing facilities started to call them and their list of customers started growing exponentially.

Now, they are a profitable company with fifty employees and more than forty-five customers. They are handling about 400 to 500 tonnes of recycling material per month and aim to reach the thousand mark soon. They need capital to grow, since their venture is capital-intensive. And that is why Luis applied to the Unreasonable Institute, to spread his idea and look for interesting opportunities.

'Since we started in September 2009, we have already increased Mexico's recycling rate by introducing recycling programmes with more than forty-five customers—from small schools to big corporations. We have educated almost 5000 people and have diverted from landfills about 1900 tonnes of waste, prevented 31,502 trees from being cut down, saved 1,22,57,046 gallons [about 4.6 crore litres] of water and 96,70,000 kWh of energy.'

They have been awarded their first landfill concession with a period of thirty years. This will allow them to handle 300 tonnes of waste per day. They are reaching the one-million-dollar mark in revenue and had reached break-even by the eighth month of operations.

'We know our business model can be easily replicated and that demand exists not only in Mexico but in most of the LatAm countries.'

> 'One of the things I really love about working in YoReciclo is that every time I go home in the evening and see my son, I know that I am making a better place for him. It is very fulfilling and keeps me motivated to try harder.'

YoReciclo caught the eye of the Unreasonable Institute and Luis became an Unreasonable Fellow, 2011.

Is there a plan to expand the venture to other parts of Mexico, or maybe even beyond Mexico?

'Definitely. We want that when people think about recycling, they think of YoReciclo. For that to happen, we need to have a presence in several countries around the world. We are starting pilot plants in other cities of Mexico to see how the market behaves. We have already talked to people in Guatemala and Columbia and it has been very interesting to talk with these mentors and investors and see their perspectives.'

They receive a lot of encouragement from mentors and investors, who have shown interest in YoReciclo's work. The biggest challenge they face at the moment is funding, but they are sure they will get through. Sometimes, they have to decline the biggest orders they get, because of lack of means to complete the orders. They need more machinery, better transportation system and manpower—everything that can be taken care of with proper funding.

'But slowly, the company is becoming stronger; our financial statements are better. The banks are also showing more trust in us, but their interest rates are crazy!'

They are creating both wealth and impact. Through all of this, we have seen that Luis' story has been one of decisions. What has been on his mind, all through this? What has been his personal philosophy, the driving force behind him?

'Follow your heart, trust your gut and have faith—that's all you need.'

Never settling for anything you are not fully satisfied with is the way to go. There aren't many things a person needs to be successful. Luis believes that there are five elements to do good work as a team. One needs to be honest and have very strong values. One needs to be a team player. Persistency is a crucial requirement; in start-ups and even corporates, there are always ups and downs—everybody has to face that. One needs to be smart, good at what one does. And it is probably a little underestimated but a sense of humour is an important factor. It is often the way you look at things that decides how you feel about them. Perspective can make all the difference.

Creating harmony at the workplace is very important. Luis

always cracks a joke at the end of meetings, however serious the matter they had just discussed may be. They are surrounded by people who have a good sense of humour and it makes working together a pleasant experience.

Has Luis ever considered an alternate world, where he is not in the recycling business?

'Yes! I keep making this silly promise to myself, and I don't know if it's good for my family or not, but Mexico, right now, is living through a very difficult period of time because of the drug cartels and corruption. I believe that if I were not in recycling, I would definitely try to find ways to help in solving the problems that Mexico is facing at the moment.'

Luis might consider getting involved in education or security—or maybe even a mixture of both—to make Mexico a better place. It's very hard to live in a place without feeling safe there.

Right now, Luis is content with the impact he is having on the society and the work his venture is doing. He has always followed his gut and done whatever he felt like doing, and believes strongly in having faith and following one's passion.

'If you're in a place where the work you do is not fulfilling, I don't know what you are doing there. If you have a feeling, the desire of doing something, just go for it. Live your life and enjoy it. It's a very short life, won't last forever.'

## What's New?

In September 2012, Luis Duarte resigned as COO and COB of YoReciclo.

Luis left the company on a firm financial footing, with a strong growth trajectory, but over 2012, he felt he needed to move on to a different challenge and continue his vision of creating social and environmental impact elsewhere. It was a tough decision, but one he felt he needed to make.

He has since joined the team at the Gary Community Investment Company (GCIC) in Colorado, and serves as the project facilitator. The GCIC is a new for-profit impact investment firm targeting innovative business creation and investment partnerships. As ever, in this new role, Luis' integrity and thorough 'unreasonableness' is shining through!

# 10

# INVEST IN GOOD

SHIVANI SIROYA

Shivani Siroya is a United Nations economist turned investment banker turned social entrepreneur. Her venture InVenture is the first global micro-investing platform, which has demonstrated an innovative use of mobile technology to provide a credit-scoring and a reporting platform to financial-services institutions and underserved micro-entrepreneurs in emerging countries. Their basic model consists of funds raised through individual investors through their web portal, and invested not as loans but as 'micro-equity' in small but potentially scalable businesses in underserved areas. They work on a profit-sharing basis with the investor and investee and use their award-winning InSight mobile tracking system to gather daily financial data to deliver credit scores and performance analytics on investments. InVenture has pioneered a standardized credit-scoring system

for unbanked individuals to qualify for financing—
something more than 270 crore individuals lack. They
then provide financial literacy, accounting and credit
scoring through InSight. The data captured by this
mobile application enables services around education,
financial metrics and partnerships to revolutionize the
low-income financial-services industry. Fundamentally,
InVenture's focus on 'numbers' and support for a micro-
equity-based model enables higher levels for business
growth and aims to create a strong and vibrant small
business sector, providing employment and income
to a large number of people in the developing world.

THE PETITE young woman standing in front of me was Shivani Siroya, founder of InVenture Fund, one of the world's fastest-growing micro-investing platforms and a pioneer using mobile technologies for enabling micro-investments in small businesses in developing nations.

I was soon to learn that this high-energy young woman (well into her late twenties, she informed me gently upon my impertinent probing!) had roots in Rajasthan, India, acquired a master's in public health from Columbia University, worked at the United Nations in New York and then as an investment banker in Los Angeles. She was now using all this experience from the international development, public health and investment banking worlds to build one of the most unique funds in the world of development finance.

Shivani's story spans two countries—India and the US—but starts in Rajasthan. Shivani's family, going back at least four generations, calls Udaipur its home. This is where she grew up, and where most of her extended family lives. This is where her father started his journey in life, a journey that would take him across continents—from India to the US—and that would take him across careers—from physics to finance.

'I must tell you something more about Dad,' says Shivani. 'He had polio. My grandparents had three children before him, who had all died. Dad was the only survivor. His polio was contained in one leg, but there were a lot of problems in his childhood. His attacks paralysed him multiple times . . . It was incredible what my grandfather and uncles did for him. They never made him feel helpless or even inferior in any way. They somehow instilled the confidence in him to do whatever he wanted in life. This is what brought him on his own to the United States . . .'

Shivani's paternal grandfather was a bank manager in Udaipur and a respected member of the local community. A strong believer in education, he always wanted his son— Shivani's father—to study physics. Shivani's father did eventually end up getting a master's in physics in Udaipur— mainly perhaps to appease his strong-willed father! However, his passion was finance and, eventually, with his father's blessing, he left his relatively comfortable life in Udaipur to find his way to the United States, where he enrolled at the University of California, Los Angeles (UCLA). Within a short period of time, however, he realized he had underestimated the costs of the education and could no longer afford to continue. He dropped out to find work to survive. He found a job at a light-bulb manufacturing plant in LA. His dexterity and efficiency in putting together light bulbs impressed his American boss, who immediately promoted him to the post of supervisor. The money was good, and he could now send some home for his family. Eventually, though, he had saved enough to give his finance education another attempt. Since US schools were expensive, he enrolled for an MBA at the University of Ottawa in Canada, and got his start in finance. Just after the completion of his course, however, he got news that his father had been in an accident. He rushed back to India, where destiny crossed his path with that of his future wife.

In the same Rajasthan hospital where his father was admitted, a young lady doctor was treating another elderly gentleman. She was efficient, capable and very confident. The elderly gentleman was very impressed with her and was determined to make a match for his nephew, with this exceptional young woman. He was the brother of Grandfather Siroya—also in the same hospital at the same time. The nephew, of course, was the (then!) young Mr Siroya, Shivani's father, newly returned from the US. The introductions happened in the hospital ward and, one week of discreet meetings, in between work hours at the hospital, was enough for the young couple to agree to a wedding and tie the knot.

'I think the main thing that impressed my dad about Mom was her confidence, and that she had her own job, was determined to make her own career . . . this was pretty rare in the India of those days!'

Shivani's father and mother both tried to make something of themselves in their young careers in the land of opportunity. They were both struggling and not very rich in a very expensive country (when you converted the rupees into dollars). Shivani was born in the US but at the age of eleven months, she was dispatched back to Udaipur, to her grandparents, to be taken care of. 'You know, looking back, it was pretty strange. I grew up till the age of six in my grandparents' house. I really thought my grandparents were my parents!'

Shivani grew to be close to her family—cousins, uncles,

aunts in India—and even after going to study in the US, continued to regularly visit them in Rajasthan.

'I remember snippets of my childhood after I was taken back to the US to my parents. What strikes me is how open my parents were. They always did everything in front of me, discussed all issues openly, treated me like an adult from a very young age. I even remember them having fights in front of me, openly. I used to try to help out and try to reason with them with well-thought-out arguments . . . I was seven!' She laughs. 'We were pretty close, the three of us. And they raised me to be very open, very honest.

'We weren't very rich at all. So my parents would often have to work on weekends, but they took me with them. So I would go off with my mom to the hospital, or with my dad to his bank . . . I remember being put in a cubicle and looking at screens full of numbers and graphs. I guess now they were trading operations my father was working on! It was actually pretty fun. I think, as a kid, if you are treated like an adult, there is nothing like it. I would just go around talking to everyone very seriously, this little seven- or eight-year-old . . . ha ha. I remember earnestly talking to patients standing by my mother's side, imitating her, admonishing the patients, "Did you check your glucose levels?"'

Shivani attended the United Nations International School in New York. By design, the curriculum emphasized learning about different cultures, histories from different points of view.

'I remember an essay we were told to write. It was about the Roman Empire. We were asked to provide our own individual stance on it. It was intimidating at first! What did I know to comment on an entire civilization? But then I decided to write this as a speech—an entire speech from the point of view of Julius Caesar! It was insane!' She laughs.

She credits the pedagogy for developing her sense of understanding and empathy, and teaching her about interacting with others and communicating effectively. 'We had lots of engagement—the teachers were never satisfied if we just had the information. They wanted us to talk about it, to debate it, to look at different angles and perspectives. For instance, I remember we learnt World War I many times over—each time from a different country's perspective!'

In school Shivani grew interested in biology, and her father—as many Indian parents do!—suggested she become a doctor. However, she grew out of her biology phase and decided she wanted to do something more creative.

'I had a phase when I suddenly wanted to become a fashion designer. And then another when I decided my calling was as a shoe designer. Whatever I wanted, I would generally throw myself wholeheartedly into it. So when I decided to become a shoe designer, I created a portfolio with 100 shoe designs . . .' Then came the next phase of trying to become an editor, then a publisher. 'Always a creative career of some sort. I never imagined I would become a businesswoman!'

Her school had made her interested in the United Nations and, eventually, she decided that would be her goal—to work for that mammoth organization. She went to Wesleyan University in Connecticut, and studied government and economics. However, her usual way of doing things—throwing herself head first into anything that interested her—worked not so well. She ended up taking too many courses—more than nine a semester at some stage—and also wanted to have as much fun as possible. 'I ended up not doing well in some of them, and my dad became concerned. He pulled me out of Wesleyan in Connecticut, where I was staying on my own, away from my mom and dad—and brought me back for a year to attend a semester in New York University.'

It worked and young Shivani found her focus again. She was back in Wesleyan University the following year, where she met Professor Melanie Price, who was teaching the government class. She was a big influence on the young Shivani, always encouraging her to link the theoretical concepts taught in class to the 'real world' outside. 'She taught me to think. She taught me to understand why I did the things I did—why take government or economics? What is it that I really wanted to accomplish?' Shivani realized that the discipline itself did not matter as much as the path in between. Where did the path lead? 'I did not know where the path led, at that stage.' She smiles. 'But I knew I didn't have to take only economics, or only medicine.' She eventually applied to the master's programme in public health at the University of Columbia, New York. This was a heady mix of public policy, medicine and economics.

'You know, if you look at my résumé, you will find that there is something or the other that I have done previously that contributes in some significant way to the building of InVenture Fund . . . It's funny how things work out! You are a product of everything that you experience. In my case, my first influences were my parents. My mom—a gynaecologist and endocrinologist—barely charges her poor patients at her clinic.

Her main reward is to spend time with them and make them better. My dad looks at things from a different perspective—the systems perspective. He looks at finance and logic and paths towards outcomes. I am a product of them both!'

Shivani interned at the United Nations Population Fund. 'I really thought that I was set in my path. This is what I would stick to—you know, health economics, probably get my PhD, then carry on working on these issues. I really thought I was going to become one of those UN people!'

But a woman there—Eva Wiseman—changed the trajectory of Shivani's life. She was her boss, and she had assigned Shivani to work on what Shivani considered rather boring work, making models in Microsoft Excel, working with lots of data. This was all from behind a desk, and the young Shivani was more enthusiastic of being in the field, being more 'hands-on'. But Eva had previously been an investment banker and wanted Shivani to understand the numbers, to internalize the rich story the data told.

'I still remember her words. She told me, "People don't use data, when they are talking of policy, or making big changes in systems. I want you to understand the power behind the numbers. I want you to really use the power. And then go into the field and use this power. Use costing models, show people how much each action costs and how much it is worth . . ."' remembers Shivani. 'And that's what I did.'

She soon realized that, in the field, this viewpoint did not go down easily. No one would talk to her about cost and benefit; they all wanted to pitch their latest million-dollar idea to get a grant or two sanctioned.

'I was all about detail. I was thinking about daily effects, how to quantify the changes of any policy action to the quality of life. Results. Outcomes. That was it! And this was not happening in the field.'

This was a jolt to Shivani. She realized that if she stayed with the UN, she would become complacent. She was disillusioned with the results of the work, but wasn't sure she could not work for the UN. What else was there that she could do? Then at that time, a chance encounter introduced her to Acumen Fund. At the time, in 2007, Acumen Fund was not the known name that it is today. It was a two-year-old impact-investment fund just about the time when the words 'impact investment' were becoming more common. It thereafter became known for pioneering an interesting mix of venture-capital and grant-funding models that it used to fund 'market-based' development initiatives.

For Shivani, this seemed very interesting—it seemed to have the right mix of finance, public health and policy, and development work that she wanted. It would combine her skills, and seemed a great way ahead for her career. However, she soon got bad news: Acumen does not hire anyone for the profile she wanted without an MBA degree.

Shivani was disappointed but her high energy and good spirits soon returned and she turned to a different job track— investment banking, of the more traditional variety. She moved to Los Angeles and worked with Citigroup, and then with Health Net. She was exposed to the world of mergers and acquisitions.

She also spent more time with her future husband, who was

an entertainment business lawyer, working in the LA area. On the work side, Shivani knew what the job demanded and did it well: Excel models, putting together pitch decks for deals, talking about the strategic aspects and so forth. The work itself was interesting enough but, gradually, Shivani yearned for more 'value'. She did not think what she was doing was having as much impact as she would have liked. At the UN, despite all the problems, she still felt there were many people with excellent intentions, trying to the best of their capacities. In the investment-banking world, the environment was fast paced but she often felt directionless, and did not feel like her work was making any positive difference to the world.

Her boyfriend/future husband offered advice: 'You're not happy because you are not making yourself happy. Quit blaming others, and do what you have to do to make yourself happy!'

Shivani introspected and realized that she had been progressively becoming unhappier for one year. She decided to quit, without having a clear plan ahead.

'Everyone had suggestions and advice to offer! Dad wanted me to again consider becoming a doctor. I liked people, I liked biology and medicine—seemed the logical choice, again! Chetan, my boyfriend, wanted me to think about going into public health . . .'

In Shivani's heart, she was looking for a way for microfinance and health to come together. The seeds of an idea had been germinating for a while, about how these two critical facets of development could come together, and now she had a lot of time to think about it seriously.

She consulted her previous boss at the UN—James Rogan. Could something like a mix of microfinance and health work? What could she do?

James was enthusiastic and had many ideas. Shivani hopped on to the first flight from LA to New York to discuss this.

'I had read everything I could about public health and healthcare in the developing world and microfinance. But these were two different worlds . . .'

Another issue close to her heart was micro-investments. From her experience with the United Nations Population Fund, she had become frustrated with the way NGOs operated. Also, she had come face-to-face with the world of microfinance, which involved giving small loans to micro-entrepreneurs to fund their businesses.

'The average loan size is still just around US$300. These loans typically have to be repaid within one year, and are usually at a fixed somewhat high interest rate. SMEs [small and medium enterprises] are key to job creation—they consist of 68 per cent of the GDP in the States and only 32 per cent in developing countries. In the developing countries, there is a "missing middle", a real big gap in funding between small loans and venture capital.

'More than $64 billion has been invested as debt to date by MFIs . . .' Shivani says. 'Microcredit is good. But for communities to be lifted out of poverty, for businesses to grow big and entrepreneurs to start employing their neighbours, we need an equity or quasi-equity instrument . . .'

Shivani's idea was to enable micro-investment. Micro-venture capital. For investors to be partners rather than lenders in businesses. The basic premise of her idea was to identify 'top performers' who had a track record of success in repaying micro-loans, and take them to the next level. Provide them larger amounts as an investment closer to 'equity' than 'debt' that would enable them to scale their business. She was thinking of unit investments of about US$15,000 rather than the typical sub-$1000 loans that MFIs offered. A key to this micro-venture-capital model would be reliable and cost-effective tracking of performance of the micro-entrepreneur and timely training and mentorship for business growth.

This was a significant departure from the way most MFIs worked, and Shivani needed some encouragement to proceed. James Rogan was extremely supportive and encouraged her to go ahead and try the concept out. Over the subsequent years, he would continue to act as a mentor and an invaluable supporter of InVenture.

Shivani decided to go to India to test her idea. But she quickly realized that, despite her family's presence in Rajasthan, she did not have any expertise on the ground to run the kind of pilot she had in mind. Then, she talked to Kocie, a friend who ran an MFI called Key Credit Microfinance in Ghana. Kocie agreed to help pilot Shivani's idea under her supervision in Ghana. At the time, Kocie was getting many proposals to pilot different types of development concepts in collaboration with Key Credit from different development organizations, including Kiva, a very large and reputed name in microfinance, but she was refusing them all. At the time, she never mentioned to Shivani why her particular project had been accepted.

'Only much later, when I was better established and present in four other countries, did Kocie come back to me with a reason as to why she had allowed me to pilot with her in Ghana—she did not feel most large organizations initiated projects for the right reasons. The underlying motive was always to grow business, meet more and more ambitious targets. In my case, Kocie thought my motive was clear—to help people directly.'

So in January 2010, InVenture Fund officially started, with their first three customers. They were vetted by Kocie, from her MFI network. Shivani's model was in action!

Meanwhile, she was still working at her day job at Health Net, managing a very hectic schedule. Nights, early mornings, weekends—all were consumed by InVenture, talking to Kocie, learning what was working, building and refining the model further.

The name 'InVenture' was given to the venture during a Skype call with James Rogan. They were in different time zones, and discussing online (with James having a drink at home). Shivani felt that the name of the venture should contain the words micro, venture or equity in some form. She came up with 'InVenture' but James did not like it. They came up with different names, and built up a list. 'InVenture' was just kept on as a placeholder, but over time it grew on Shivani until she just never changed it. It just remained.

The first group of collaborators working with the project used to dial in from Los Angeles, Washington DC, Ghana, Michigan, even Europe—refining the model, having long discussions about what should be done next.

'James kept pushing it. Many times, I would be tired after my day job at Health Net, and there was a danger of it remaining just an idea . . . but James used to ask me, "What are you doing about it today?" InVenture Fund would never have happened without him!'

Eventually, full-time staff emerged—Tom, the portfolio manager, and Jen, marketing and operations. They were connections through the LA microfinance network, and with whom Shivani had debated this idea endlessly before. 'Jen was between jobs at the time, and only joined as this was an interesting opportunity before the next job. Then she never left! Later on, Bonnie, another friend from Wesleyan with whom I was always talking about doing something together, came on board.' It was a perfect fit and the team worked furiously to get the venture off the ground.

'By the way, in case you are wondering "Why LA?" it has to do with personal reasons—my husband is an entertainment lawyer and all his clients are here . . . I decided not to move too far . . . But again, it's a funny world. At the time no one was doing microfinance in LA, but now it is becoming interesting in LA too.'

Shivani and Chetan, her long-time boyfriend, tied the knot in December 2010, shortly before the Unreasonable Institute.

Shivani got seed funding of US$40,000 from a programme of the Chile government called Start-up Chile and also was supported by the Echoing Green foundation in New York. Subsequently, she raised a total of half a million dollars over two equity rounds in 2011 and 2012 to build the InVenture team and technology platform. 'The source of funding for the

SMEs we fund is direct from individual "investors" from our web platform,' she explains.

The InVenture model has evolved rapidly since the early days. The InVenture team has examined four separate types of models: buyout in Ghana, profit-sharing in India, cooperative in Mali and step down in Mexico. 'A straight revenue-sharing model won out,' says Shivani. In addition to the basic premise of providing an equity-like instrument to fund micro-entrepreneurs, their model now includes two key features: credit scores and accounting tools to individuals. 'This is very important, especially as we deal with people who lack access to formal financial services,' explains Shivani. 'We're pioneers in the use of mobile technology to track this. We built a tool called InSight through which entrepreneurs and investors track daily revenue, costs and generate analytics report at the back end . . .'

The InVenture model works on crowdfunding, whereby 'InVestors'—individuals mostly in the US and Europe—create, account and commit a pool of money to invest in one or more small or medium businesses in underserved parts of the world. The InVenture web interface allows the investors to study profiles and track records of potential investees. They can also track daily performance metrics of each investment they make. Since this is not a formal equity investment, the returns are in the form of a percentage of the profit made, which can then be reinvested. The data from daily transactions is generated via a proprietary mobile platform called InSight, which gathers it from investees via regular SMS updates.

In addition, InVenture also partners with local MFIs and

consultants to provide business expertise and advice for their investees. InVenture charges about 5 per cent of profits from each investee to reinvest in various community health and other projects with social impact for the communities it operates in.

'Five years from now, I want to look back on having created something of lasting value . . . a suite of financial products, both crowdfunding and equity models, products that are flexible and customizable for the client. Maybe I am crazy but in five years I want to look back and see all the thousands of jobs we have enabled that our investees would be creating. I want to see consolidation happening, value from economies of scale being unlocked. Instead of twelve small, inefficient tile makers in one village, three big, efficient ones that would compete better with external competition, create strong value in terms of income and jobs for the local community . . . We would be creating a strong small and medium business sector here!'

The biggest challenge Shivani and her team face is always linked to the data. Or rather the lack of data. Unlike the more mature markets of the West, underserved financial markets are characterized by people who have no documented credit history. It becomes impossible for financial institutions to trust them. One of the big innovations from InVenture is InSight that enables micro-entrepreneurs to log data and, over time, build up credit scores and histories. From the entrepreneur's point of view, this opens up different sources of funding for business expansion. From the investor's or financial institution's perspective, they have greater transparency and a clear idea of the financial performance metrics of the business.

This rather cool mobile text-messaging tool allows

everyone in whom InVenture invests to use a basic cell phone to balance their books and better understand the financial health of their business. Each day they text their expenses and revenue and, in the process, also gain better knowledge of what is needed to succeed in their business. InVenture, at the back end, plugs this information into an advanced algorithm, which calculates and publishes the credit score—a metric hitherto unavailable to the vast majority of the micro-entrepreneurs. This is the crux of it—how this tool gives developing entrepreneurs the chance to expand with quasi-equity funding, to employ more of their neighbours and to lift their communities out of poverty.

There are a lot of processes involved in this, which InVenture has to manage. Every day is a challenge in getting all this done—'Imagine tracking collection of money across multiple geographies, with many small ventures in the portfolio . . . Putting the processes in place is a slow and difficult task, a real challenge . . .' says Shivani.

InVenture has hired locally, in each area it operates. The mobile infrastructure behind their InSight platform is inherently scalable, and one of the big reasons behind their success so far. The key to making the model work is excellent working partnerships with local agencies, local MFIs.

Shivani has an infectious enthusiasm. 'I always have an ability to make everyone excited about the things I am excited about.' She laughs. 'And I use way too many exclamation points. I get so excited!!!'

InVenture is growing—from the current state of providing

InSight services to two lenders and five NGO partners (who each have a portfolio of businesses and relationships with their set of micro-entrepreneurs), Shivani is targeting 40,000 end users on the InSight platform in the next twelve months.

'For 2016, we plan to reach 30 million [3 crore] micro-borrowers across emerging economies using InSight . . .' says Shivani, with a completely straight face. 'Now, *that* would be some feat!' she bursts out with energy.

At present, Shivani and her team have their hands full, executing the key tasks to achieving their ambitious targets—establishing relationships with ten banks and MFIs, and hiring experienced resources across geographies. 'We also hope to form partnerships in the different geographies. For example, we have one on the cards in Kenya happening soon . . .' she tapers off.

In a somewhat surprising irony, InVenture has also found success in New York City, where their projects in the South Bronx have found many takers. 'What is interesting also is that even in the US, people seem to prefer to use text messaging on our InSight mobile platform rather than any app on a smartphone. I guess people like simplicity, regardless of which country they are from!'

Shivani Siroya is changing the world, one small business at a time. InVenture is combining technology and information to unlock financial access in very underserved markets.

'Social impact is baked into my model,' she explains sweetly. 'It is hard for me not to do good!'

And I, for one, am not arguing!

## What's New?

I spoke to Shivani again in January 2013, asking for an update since our first interview.

'I'm still married!' she said, laughing.

Nice! Good update! But some big things had changed at InVenture. Fundamentally, their vision remained the same— to enable access to financial literacy and capital so that small industry can grow and lift communities out of poverty—but their focus had undergone an important change: increasingly, they were focused on InSight, their pioneering mobile-based accounting and financial-monitoring application. So much so that this product had become their core offering, and rather than being a lender or raiser of money from the crowd, InVenture was now a service provider to other financial institutions, 'renting out' the use of their InSight solution.

This change started in December 2011. At this time, the first version of InSight had been built and the second version of InSight was released to 250 clients in India. These clients were part of the Chennai pilot of InSight. This was an important time for the young company, as one meeting was going to change their business almost completely.

At the December 2011 meeting of the board of directors of InVenture, Shivani advocated a complete change of strategy. Rather than spread their resources thin across managing a crowdfunding website, a lending platform with direct commitment to and from borrowers and a mobile product, she proposed they exit from the first two businesses and focus completely on InSight, their mobile product. Her contention: lack of focus was inevitable if the team continued to divide their attention across all three at once. With only four core team members at this stage, her point was well received by the board. To make her case, she had done her homework.

The board heard feedback from different stakeholders who were specially called for the meeting. Also, in the month prior to the meeting, Shivani and her team had painstakingly called up multiple people within eighty-four financial institutions in India, sent more than two thousand emails to bring out one common point: for *everyone* in the sector, access to reliable data about borrowers—especially data for borrowers *after* the loan was disbursed—was a pain point. And importantly, that these organizations were willing to pay to get data to reduce their pain! InSight was a product that specifically addressed the data problem. If InVenture, via InSight, could provide data that empowered lending, it would add value, tremendous value, to the financial ecosystem at the bottom of the pyramid.

'We didn't have to change our vision. Financial inclusion, opportunity and choice—what enables that? One is access and the other is education, financial literacy. InSight encompassed both those values—we should be focusing on that. We didn't have to be the lender or the crowdfunding platform . . . There were other people who were doing that!'

The board unanimously supported Shivani's plan. It was

a momentous day: in one surgical stroke, the company had changed. The perfect pivot?

'It was a bold move.' Shivani smiles. 'I am very happy that we made this shift. Many people are scared to change track so rapidly—they would rather keep running with a model that is not working, trying to convince themselves that it is working. I think it is better to be honest, see quickly what is working, what is not and then act, based on the data in front of you.'

How did Shivani spot the trend in the data in front of her in those weeks leading up to December 2011?

'You know, the idea itself was excellent—to be the crowdsourcing platform, to be the lender, manage borrowers and portfolio on the ground, and then have a technology platform on the mobile for the data. But even apart from the challenge of doing everything with a small start-up team, there are some fundamental truths. For example, for crowdsourcing, we gave donors in the US amazing visibility—unprecedented—into the inner workings of the business their money was going into. They would log into the daily cash transactions, revenues, costs and profits of the businesses in India they were helping. But most users who invested were not interested in this. They only cared for the story, not in the inner workings . . .'

InVenture raised a total of US$70,000 from the online crowdfunding platform, with the average user in the US putting in fifty US dollars.

'To persist with this model would have meant me personally having to focus heavily on the donor side. There are other organizations doing that—and outsourcing the actual operational work in the field. Personally, I was more interested in what happened to the money after it came . . . so I couldn't see InVenture scaling with the crowdsourcing part.'

So, InVenture pulled the plug on its crowdfunding platform, raising a few eyebrows in the process. But their InSight platform was gathering momentum. Over January to April 2012, InSight was tested and refined on more clients, and the core product offering made simpler and better. It now understood exactly what users needed. 'No language, only keywords in SMS. Works on voice also—IVR—which is free! Also, in a country of so many languages but so much illiteracy, we realized that numbers is the universal language. And this all went into InSight . . .' quips Shivani. InSight built in incentives and feedback loops—using data from savings and budget reports, income statements, loan balance statements—to empower end users and at the same time provide crucial data to lenders. InSight was made to now include a strong back end—a web dashboard for financial institutions to track their portfolios. 'You can do so many things from there! Pre-approve loans, pre-empt defaults, there is an algorithm for credit scoring . . .' says Shivani. In May 2012, the first lender institution—Bengaluru-based Vistaar—started paying for data from Insight. Three other large non-banking financial companies (NBFCs) followed suit, including Muthoot Housing Finance and MyMela.

'The journey from December 2011 felt almost like starting a brand-new company in one year,' recalls Shivani. Today, more than 6500 clients are using the InSight product in India. It has an incredible 85 per cent retention rate—so people who use the product seldom leave it. Along with the core data,

InVenture now also provides workshops and guidance sessions to customers on how best to make use of their data. Both at the business and household level, clients are discovering value in the product.

InVenture has stayed outside of conventional microfinance by design. NBFCs are using InSight for portfolio tracking and lead generation. At the macro level, the data is also uncovering interesting trends.

'For example, we can see that many tile makers, say, in a region are buying raw materials. Bulk purchasing may reduce the costs . . . and an NGO working in this area may be interested in efficiencies like that! . . . That is the type of service that InSight's macro is also now enabling across sectors.'

Another big thing on the horizon is connecting unique identification numbers (UID) with Insight's credit-rating score. 'That would really put everyone on the map,' says Shivani enthusiastically.

Other countries are also now catching on to Insight, and there is a large demand for the product. InVenture has learnt its lessons, though, and has explicitly avoided setting up its own infrastructure in other countries—they operate on a licensing model, where currently organizations in Kenya, Mexico, Brazil and Uganda are being offered six-monthly subscriptions to InSight and other support services to make it work. So that's another revenue stream!

To fund their growth, InVenture has, to date, raised slightly above half a million dollars, with investments from individual angels, USAID DIV, Vodafone and Mumbai Angels.

The team has now nine members: Shivani, three engineers

and five operational people, based in Santa Monica, Mumbai and Bengaluru. An interesting thing about the organization is that the leaders in business development, operations, technology and finance are all women, all under thirty!

Shivani giggles. 'Every time we walk into the offices of a large Indian financial institution, waiting to face a boardroom of fifty-year-old Indian men with moustaches, perhaps asking themselves who these women are!'

Asha Rani, the director of products, was hired from Janalakshmi. Dasassami Mudlee, leading business development, comes from Intellicap. All in all, they make a formidable team!

Shivani talks easily and fluently of her journey. Where will InVenture be in three years' time?

'Three years is a long time. By then, we might have gone full circle and gotten back into lending again!' She grins. 'But we are very positive at present. We believe we have the right set of tools, enabling both our clients—and us!—to take the right decisions.'

# ACKNOWLEDGEMENTS

WE MET each other at a TEDx event organized by IIM Calcutta in July 2012, where we were both speakers. That was where Myshkin told me about the idea for this book, and also told me that he had already recorded the interviews. He was discussing this with me because I had been writing and had published three novels by then and Myshkin seemed to think that I knew what I was doing. I answered the questions he had and he promised he'd contact me if he needed anything else. When he later did contact me, he said (and I'm quoting his exact words here), 'I am not a professional writer! I need discipline (or someone to discipline me?) to get down and get this done in time. I have already procrastinated for six months.'

This was July. I got him in touch with my publishers and everything was sorted out. Myshkin promised to send in the completed book to us by the end of August. Next time he came up for air (he's a workaholic and extremely devoted to his venture, Biosense), it was already December. That's when I jumped in, and took up his offer of co-authoring the book, which he had proposed in July. And what fun it has been!

To begin with, we would like to thank our families

for their constant support and faith in us. The folks at Penguin—especially Vaishali Mathur and Shruti Narain—for their patience and cooperation and for having confidence in our work.

We would like to thank all the Fellows for their cooperation throughout the process, starting with the initial interviews till the approval of completed documents and tolerating the constant barrage of mails we send their way. Nat, Jennifer, Ties, Donna, Sanga, Saba, Luis, Shivani, Raj and Anna—you've been amazing and we love you all. We are also grateful to the Unreasonable Institute for giving us the permission to use the information on their website and their records for various facts and figures mentioned in the book.

Guruji, for the strength he provides and the shoulder he lends, through the darkest of times.

A special thanks to everyone at TEDxIIMC 2012. That's where it all began and we'll always be grateful.